Great Church Fights

Leslie B. Flynn

This book is designed for your personal reading pleasure and profit. It is also designed for group study. A leader's guide with helps and hints for teachers is available from your local Christian bookstore or from the publisher at $1.25.

a division of SP Publications, Inc.
WHEATON, ILLINOIS 60187

ACKNOWLEDGEMENTS

All quotations in this book are used by permission of the copyright holders to whom we express our thanks. The author and editors are grateful for permission to use quotations from the following books and periodical:
The Letter to the Romans, translated by William Barclay, © 1958 by Westminster Press, Philadelphia.
Church Fights, by Speed Leas and Paul Kitlaus, © 1973, Westminster Press, Philadelphia.
The Acts of the Apostles, by G. Campbell Morgan, © 1924, Fleming H. Revell Co., Old Tappan, N. J.; *A Turned-On Church In An Uptight World*, © 1971 by Peter Wagner, Zondervan Publishing House, Grand Rapids, Mich.; *Look Out the Pentecostals Are Coming*, by C. Peter Wagner, © 1973, Creation House, Carol Stream, Ill.; *Man at the Top*, by Richard Wolff, © 1969, Tyndale House Publishers, Wheaton, Ill.; "Integration's Uncertain Trumpet," article in *Evangelical Newsletter*, September 26, 1975, Evangelical Foundation, Philadelphia.

Bible quotations are from the King James Version unless otherwise noted. Other quotations are from *The Holy Bible: An American Translation* by William F. Beck (BECK), published by Leader Publishing Company, New Haven, Mo., *The Living Bible* (LB), © Tyndale House Publishers, Wheaton, Ill.; *The New American Standard Bible* (NASB), © 1971, The Lockman Foundation, La Habra, Calif.; *The New International Version: New Testament* (NIV), © 1973, The New York Bible Society International; the *New Testament in Modern English* by J. B. Phillips (PH), © 1958, The Macmillan Company. All quotations used by permission.

Library of Congress Catalog Card Number: 76-14645
ISBN: 0-88207-743-0

VICTOR BOOKS
A division of SP Publications, Inc.
P.O. Box 1825 • Wheaton, Ill. 60187

CONTENTS

THE AUTHOR / Leslie B. Flynn has pastored the Grace Conservative Baptist Church of Nanuet, New York since 1949. He is a graduate of Moody Bible Institute (pastor's course), Wheaton College (B.A.), Eastern Baptist Theological Seminary (B.D.), the University of Pennsylvania (M.A. in philosophy), and received a D.D. from Conservative Baptist Theological Seminary of Denver in 1963. He has been an instructor in journalism at Nyack Missionary College and has long been active as an author. His other books under the Victor label include *Me Be Like Jesus?*, a study in Christlike living, *19 Gifts of the Spirit*, an in-depth study of the spiritual gifts, and *Now a Word from Our Creator*, a study of the Ten Commandments for today.

To Dr. Ralph L. Keiper
whose friendship, with that of his wife, Nan, has been
most deeply valued through the years
and who suggested this series of studies

FOREWORD

A father heard a commotion in his yard and looked outside to see his daughter and several playmates in a heated quarrel. At his reprimand the daughter explained, "We're just playing church!"

To characterize God's people as wrangling malcontents is to caricature the church. Feuds, factions, fracases, and fusses—yes, the Christian Church has had its share, but the fellowship and fervent love have far exceeded the friction.

Yet, no church is exempt from crippling conflict. Even the early Church, so often idealized and idolized, had dissension. The list of apostolic churches where contention broke out reads like an ecclesiastical hall of fame. Jerusalem, Antioch, Rome, Corinth, Philippi, Thessalonica, and by implication, several others. No church escapes it entirely. The real question is: Will disagreements divide and wound the Christian Body, or will they draw the members together in deepened understanding and commitment?

Besides introductory and concluding chapters, eight instances of discord and conciliation in apostolic churches are examined. Another chapter deals with Jesus' instruction for brothers at odds with each other. The remaining chapter investigates reasons for withdrawal of fellowship.

This book does not evaluate all causes of church strife nor catalog all known remedies. It surveys ten significant New Testament episodes of strife and the measures taken to resolve them, in the hope that biblical insights and principles will help 20th-century churches turn their internal skirmishes into training grounds for victory.

With church fellowship in the spotlight today, a volume on church friction seems inappropriate. But friction wisely resolved turns into powerful coordinated action, and in the church that means moving ahead for God's glory.

1

We Need Each Other

Two porcupines in northern Canada huddled together to get warm, according to a forest folk tale. But their quills pricked each other and they moved apart. Before long they were shivering and they sidled close again. New scene; same ending. They needed each other, but they kept needling each other.

How like Christians! Through the centuries the Church, instead of majoring in communion, has often muddled in contention. Despite the halo of spirituality imagined over the apostolic church, the dust clouds of sharp collisions were equally visible. There were Paul's dispute with Barnabas, cliques' clashes at Corinth, women's contention at Philippi, and other controversies chronicled on the pages of the New Testament.

Today such accounts may not get into church records or the local papers, but every congregation experiences some dissension. As long as Christians care about the church, they will disagree on how to operate it and what to believe.

If all denominations were combined, the next generation would probably produce a new variety. The Lutherans, Episcopalians, and some others would likely come up with different names, and the Baptists would still settle for First, Second, Third, etc.!

Every congregation these days includes the traditionalist and the innovator. Tension will pulsate between those who want to maintain the status quo and those who want to branch into something new. Some yearn for traditional music; others demand modern forms. Some enjoy a fixed order of service; others prefer it unstructured. Some appreciate quiet dignity; others respond to enthusiastic handclapping. Said one pastor, "If my people decided to evangelize the town, some would advocate tract distribution and door-to-door visitation, but others would bring in church-growth experts."

The generation gap is almost measurable in some churches. The leader of a certain youth club, just turned 40, was conservative in politics and garb, and he considered himself "square." He was delighted to hear he was to have a new helper until he saw the young man's long hair and casual clothes at a Sunday service. He lamented, "I don't understand this new generation." The young helper grumbled: "He's not open to change; the club operates like it did ten years ago."

Varying viewpoints arise naturally from the basic differences between people, whether of age, race, social status, financial standing, or educational level. The real surprise is our unpreparedness for these differences.

More distressing and often disastrous are the differences stemming from ulterior motives and personality conflicts. Some men, dominated at work, throw their weight around at church. Others exploit fellow members for personal prestige, praise, or financial profit. Grievous to see are headlines which read, "Ex-Aide Sues Evangelist"; or "Church Treasurer Indicted."

Churches would find themselves flanked by controversy even if all arguments arising from personal pique could be eliminated. Churches deal with life-and-death matters in a cosmic struggle of good and evil. The church is no sedate country club. But all confrontations are not necessarily evil. Marriage counselors point out that though conflict is expected in the marriage relationship, a dispute need not be a destructive force. An argument joined with the right attitude can clarify issues, promote a better understanding of viewpoints, and fuse a decision good for both.

Similarly, all conflict in ecclesiastical life is not unhealthy *per se*. Disagreements, with their accompanying misunderstanding, hurt feelings, and competitiveness do carry the potential of destructive bitterness, but if they are properly handled through peaceable wisdom from above, they can be a constructive force for uniting the body of Christ (James 3:13-18).

The chapters following will deal with significant conflicts in the New Testament, generally in the order in which they appear in the sacred record. Consideration of the principles followed in resolving these early-church controversies should help our 20th-century churches. Out of friction can arise new love and strength in the family of God.

The Believer family

Believers are knit together in an invisible yet intimate relationship. The Apostles' Creed calls it the "communion of saints." A mission board doctrinal statement phrases it: "We believe in the spiritual unity of believers in Christ." Paul tells us: "You are all God's children by believing in Christ Jesus" (Gal. 3:26, BECK).

Two of Jesus' disciples came from diametrically opposed backgrounds. Matthew, a tax collector for the Roman government, engaged in an occupation considered traitorous by Jewish patriots. Simon, an ex-member of the Zealot party with its nationalistic passion, must have found it difficult to accept a former collaborationist such as Matthew. But Jesus prayed that they—and other believers—might be one (John 17:11). Through Jesus' redemptive work, not only Matthew and Simon but all varieties of believers are united in one Spirit. Accordingly, Paul spoke of the Christian Church as one body with Christ as Head and the believers as cooperating members.

Organizational unity of church denominations is secondary to the spiritual, organic unity of true Christians. The National Association of Evangelicals lists more than 35 different denominations among its 30,000 member churches, all confessing a common faith. Christians attending a Billy Graham rally sense a oneness with other believers, despite their varying ecclesiastical backgrounds. They sing with real significance:

We are not divided,
All one body we,
One in hope and doctrine,
One in charity.

This spiritual kinship even transcends natural relationships. Two brothers, one a Christian and the other an enthusiastic member of a fraternal organization, were touring Europe together. One day they encountered a missionary from America, and the two Christians immediately began an animated conversation on spiritual matters.

Later the club-loving brother remarked, "I didn't know you knew that missionary. Where did you meet him?" The Christian replied he had never seen the missionary before, and his brother exclaimed, "You talked like long-lost friends."

Replied the believer, "That's how we felt, because we belong to the same Lord."

One of the early and frequent names for a Christian was "brother." Since God has appointed believers to be conformed to the image of His Son so "that He might be the firstborn among many brethren" (Rom. 8:29), then all sons of God are brothers of Jesus Christ. How can we get unbrotherly to someone who is our brother?

Perhaps the most graphic use of this title was Ananias' greeting to "Brother Saul," the newly converted persecutor of Christians who had come to Damascus to imprison followers of "the way" (Acts 9:17). In later years the great apostle never forgot that greeting, mentioning it a quarter century later while relating his conversion story to the Sanhedrin (22:13). When we recall that the disciples at Jerusalem doubted Paul's sincerity, this warm greeting by Ananias is all the more remarkable (9:26). Perhaps a more generous use of "brother" in Christian salutations today would remind us that we should be exercising brotherly love in our fellowships.

At the close of a banquet attended by people from numerous evangelical persuasions, the soloist sang,

There is a sweet, sweet Spirit in this place,
And I know that it's the Spirit of the Lord.
There are sweet expressions on each face,
And I know they feel the presence of the Lord.*

Every Family Has Its Fights

A motorist asked a boy where the Reformed Church was located, and was told: "Go one block south and you'll see a church on the corner. That's the United Church. Go one block more, and you'll come on a church that's not united. That's it!"

Unity is more than a name, but the Church everywhere does have friction. Though we need each other, sometimes we needle—or slash—each other. Even Paul, strong advocate of unity that he was, found himself embroiled in personal and ecclesiastical disputes. The "church fights" recorded in the New Testament frankly acknowledge the foibles of early saints along with their good qualities.

The young church's first recorded conflict concerned the complaint of Grecians against Hebrews because their widows were neglected in the daily food apportionment (Acts 6:1-6).

Paul publicly rebuked Peter for open prejudice toward Gentile believers (Gal. 2:11-14).

Those who still believed in circumcision criticized Peter for bringing the Gospel to Gentiles (Acts 11:2-3). The same reason caused "No small dissension and disputation" between Paul and

---

the advocates of circumcision who believed this was essential to salvation (15:1-2). The simmering controversy necessitated the first church council and "much debate" among its leaders (v. 7, NASB).

A sharp disagreement between Paul and Barnabas over whether to take Mark on their second missionary journey caused their divided ministries (Acts 15:36-40).

The Corinthian church verged on a split with factions campaigning for different leaders (1 Cor. 1:11-12). This division widened when spiritual brothers went to court against each other (6:1-11), and the well-to-do declined to share their food with the poor at church "love feasts" (11:18-23).

Two factions developed at Rome over whether to eat meat associated with sacrifices to idols or to observe the sabbath (Rom. 14:1-6).

A disagreement between two prominent women at the Philippian church, Euodias and Syntyche, brought an appeal from Paul in his letter (Phil. 4:2-3). Jesus had expected such altercations and had earlier given instructions for both offending and offended parties (Matt. 5:23-24; 18:15-17).

Hints of needling among early saints crop up many times. Paul referred to the Galatians' biting and devouring one another (5:15). He exhorted the Philippians to "do everything without complaining or arguing" (2:14, NIV). James implied the presence of battles among the brethren when he asked the source of "wars and fightings among you?" (4:1) He traced this to selfish ambition and bitter jealousy in their hearts (3:14).

A lust for preeminence led church-boss Diotrephes to cast fellow brethren out of the church (3 John 9-10).

Somebody wrote,

> To dwell above with saints we love,
> That will be grace and glory.
> To live below with saints we know;
> That's another story!

Keeping Peace in the Family

Relatives have good reasons for strong relationships. Brothers who are unbrotherly are barbaric. A church family should be warm and mutually supporting. Though believers cannot always get along smoothly *with* fellow believers, neither can they get along *without* each other. A glowing coal removed from others in the fireplace will soon lose its warmth and light.

"Our church has unity—we're frozen together," joked one Christian. Hardly anyone laughed. For believers to function in friction is like a car running with a wheel scraping the fender. For believers to bitterly separate from other genuine Christians and speak of "they" as opposed to "us" is as incongruous as for a hand to consider itself independent from the heart that pumps it blood. We must beware of promoting a "many-bodies-of-Christ" stance. Rather, believers are one body, and all belong to each other.

The Spirit does not want schism, but solidarity in Christ's body. The eye has need of the ear, as does the hand of the foot. Competition cleaves the body, but care coordinates it.

Since the unity of the Spirit is a reality in Him, we do not try to originate it, but we must make every effort to extend His influence. At the start of Paul's practical exhortations in Ephesians, he urges: "endeavouring to keep the unity of the Spirit in the bond of peace" (4:3, KJV). To do so requires the graces mentioned in the preceding verse: humility, gentleness, patience, and forbearance in the face of faults which displease and even offend (v. 2).

The need for unity takes high priority in Paul's thinking. Over and over he encourages the pursuit of peace. "Live in harmony with one another" (Rom. 12:16, NIV). "If it is possible, as far as it depends on you, live at peace with everyone (v. 18). "Let us therefore follow after the things which make for peace" (14:19). "Be at peace among yourselves" (1 Thes. 5:13).

Leaders have a vital role in peacekeeping, therefore their

character should be free of belligerence, violence, quarrelsomeness, and impetuousness (1 Tim. 3:3; Titus 1:7). The Lord's servant must be kind to everyone (2 Tim. 2:24).

Paul does not push "peace at any price." Scandal, factional schism, and distortion of basic doctrine require disciplinary action, because purity in faith and conduct is essential to unity. Sometimes disfellowshiping the unrepentant party, such as at Corinth, is necessary for the peace and strength of the body members (1 Cor. 5:1-5).

Sam Shoemaker, the Episcopal preacher-author, wrote: "The coinage and cost of peace is righteousness . . .righteousness itself is a by-product of faith in God." Thus, gaining and maintaining peace in God's family requires divine help. Righteous relationships based on faith in God is the basic necessity.

God is called "the God of peace" several times (Rom. 16:20; 1 Thes. 5:23; 2 Thes. 3:16; Heb. 13:20). To the division-torn church at Corinth, Paul writes, "God is not a God of confusion, but of peace" (1 Cor. 14:33, NASB). The ultimate healer of all church rifts is the God of peace.

An American doctor traveling in Korea knew just enough of the language to get around. At a station stop an old Korean boarded the train and sat across from the doctor. He carried a large bundle in a white cloth. Soon the old Korean began to speak to the doctor, pouring out a torrent of words. The doctor replied with the only sentence he had memorized, "I do not understand Korean." The old man persisted. A second time the doctor gave his stock answer. This was repeated a third time.

In the stream of Korean words the doctor thought he had detected a somewhat familiar word. Had the old man said something about Jesus? His doubt vanished when the Korean pointed to the doctor and asked, "Yesu? Yesu?" With a smile the doctor nodded agreement, "Yesu, Yesu."

Smiling from ear to ear, the Korean opened his large bundle and proudly displayed his Korean Bible. Then he put his finger on a verse. The doctor couldn't read it, of course, but carefully figuring out the approximate place in his own Bible, he read from 1 John 3:14: "We know that we have passed out of death into life, because we love the brethren" (NASB).

The barriers of language, culture, and age fell as unity of spirit flowed between the two men. The Korean turned to another text, "Behold, how good and how pleasant it is for brethren to dwell together in unity!" (Ps. 133:1) As the train rolled along, the two believers rejoiced in warm Christian fellowship.

If two saints with such contrasting backgrounds can experience the unity of the Spirit, can not we who fellowship in the same church circles overcome lesser obstacles to enrich each other and glorify God?

No one relishes family life that reverberates with tension and feuding. Our spiritual health and fruitfulness require that we "keep the peace, brother."

2

Friction Frays the Fellowship

A deaconess was distributing communion at a New York church when she came to a minister of the denomination who was strongly opposed to women clergy. After receiving the communion, he deliberately raked his fingernails across the back of her hand, drawing blood. A viscious insult followed, confirming his hatred.

Just as we are shocked to find acrimony at the Lord's table today, so are we surprised to discover discord in the early church where all things were supposed to be held in common and shared in love.

Often we lament, "If only we could return to the good old days of the apostolic church." Yes, it does shine brightly from the distant past. We recall the believers at Jerusalem faithfully observing doctrine, fellowship, the breaking of bread, and prayer. Somehow we extend this glowing picture into a fantasy of perfection, a church without problems. But the realistic biblical account tells how the unit was shattered by internal grievance.

The Paradox of Conflict

Discord among the believers at this time seems so contradictory. The church was prospering numerically; it was basking in the afterglow of Pentecost; and the Christians shared their possessions with all.

This first rift broke out "while the disciples were increasing in number" (Acts 6:1, NASB). But a growing membership doesn't guarantee harmony. Affluence can be dangerous to churches as well as individuals, bringing complacency and false confidence. More people may mean more trouble; prosperity may produce problems. So it was here. Success created a potentially serious situation.

Only a few months before, at Pentecost, the disciples were filled with the Holy Spirit and 3,000 people were converted to Christ. By now the number had expanded to 5,000 (Acts 4:4). Jews of both Palestinian and foreign backgrounds had been molded into loving unity. But the oneness of the groups with differing cultures was threatening to come apart.

From the beginning, through the prompting of the Holy Spirit, believers pooled their resources and shared with needy brothers. This beautiful spirit of community not only displayed the remarkable fruit of their love in Christ, but demonstrated that money given to alleviate poverty is just as spiritual as funds designated for missions.

The record reads, "The multitude of them that believed were of one heart and of one soul: neither said any of them that aught of the things which he possessed was his own; but they had all things common" (4:32). According to Clarke's Commentary, some manuscripts add, "And there was no kind of difference or dissension among them."

It was this pinnacle of piety that Satan tried to undermine with a two-pronged attack. First, he tempted Ananias and Sapphira to pretend to emulate the example of others selling property and giving the money to the church. This couple withheld some of the sale price and acted as though they had contributed every bit of the proceeds. Their hypocrisy was exposed and drastically judged by the Holy Spirit through Peter.

Satan tried again to gain a foothold at the point of sacrificial sharing by stirring up dissension over the uneven distribution of this charity. So the glittering bubble of a perfect church burst with this first case of in-church feuding.

The imperfectness of even regenerate human nature makes some conflict inevitable. In any organization, ecclesiastical or secular, leadership creates a certain tension, declares Richard Wolff in *Man at the Top*. "Not every conflict is necessarily neurotic. Some is normal and healthy. The tension between what is and what ought to be—the gap between reality and ideal—is indispensable to well-being. Every challenge carries tension within itself. We do not need a tension-less state, but a challenging goal and purpose" (Tyndale House Publishers, Wheaton, Ill. 1969, p. 77).

In their book *Church Fights*, Speed Leas and Paul Kittlaus suggest that any church with no problems "would be a very dumb, shallow, and depressing kind of place." They deplore the fact that conflict is a feared "no-no," and when engaged in produces guilt feelings. On the contrary, they suggest, church people "can handle conflict and, in fact, enjoy challenging and being challenged." Churches do exist that have a history of dealing with conflicts, both large and small, "fairly and openly, and where the membership is not immobilized by a difference of opinion."

Such was the case in the Church's first recorded dispute. It faced the problem squarely and charitably, so that out of trouble came triumph.

A Murmuring

Luke, the writer of Acts, stated the situation: "When the number of disciples was increasing, the Grecian Jews among them complained against those of the Aramaic-speaking community because their widows were being overlooked in the daily distribution of food" (6:1, NIV).

Two groups were mentioned, though both were Jews. Both

worshiped Jehovah; both were loyal to Christ; both were of the same nation and blood; but their customs were different. The Greek-speaking Hebrew Christians had come under the influence of Greek culture when they or their ancestors lived outside Israel. Though the Holy City had a majority of Aramaic-speaking Hebrews, a large number of Grecian Jews lived there. Says Acts, "There were dwelling at Jerusalem Jews, devout men, out of every nation under heaven" (2:5). About 15 of those nations are mentioned (vv. 8-11).

Both groups included widows in need of material help. In the early weeks, no one lacked because possessors of lands and houses sold them and brought the proceeds to the apostles to share with the needy. But now came this strong complaint to complicate their harmony.

Was the grievance justified? Likely it was. The word *neglected,* used only here in the New Testament, means literally "to look beyond, to view amiss, overlook, slight." The imperfect tense of the verb indicates continuous action, hinting that the neglect had gone on for some time.

Was the slight intentional? Perhaps some prejudice did flare. Just as today's Sabras (Israel-born Jews) subconsciously consider themselves superior to foreign-born Jews, so Hebrews of the first century often regarded Grecian Jews as second-class citizens. Maybe the Hebrew element, in the majority and in charge, regarded their Hellenistic brethren as having only a secondary claim on their food. After all—this was Jerusalem, and these people were foreigners. So if the food was short, the Grecians may have received a smaller share.

But it seems more likely the neglect was accidental. As the church grew in numbers, it grew in need. The task of distribution became more complex, requiring more supervision than the apostles could give (4:35). In any case, the Grecian widows were slighted and the loving community was jeopardized. Action had to be taken.

Facing the Problem

Avoiding problems multiplies problems. Researchers Leas and Kittlaus say: "Where groups tend to suppress conflict, there will be an accumulation of feeling, leading toward a potentially dangerous conflict. A group in conflict can be like a pressure cooker as the heat (conflict) increases, the pressure builds up. The more pressure, the greater the explosion if the pressure is not abated. . . . Pressure can build up causing a large explosion over a rather minor conflict. . . . For example, we encountered a conflict where a minister lost his church over the question whether the memorial plaque for the church's members who have died would be in the narthex or in the social hall" (*Church Fights,* pp. 47-48).

Some church leaders might have glossed over the widows' complaint. "Don't be bothered by so trivial a matter as material things. You should not be concerned with meat that perishes, but rather concentrate on meat which endures to eternal life." Not the apostles.

Accepting the indirect criticism—for procedures of alms-distribution were under their jurisdiction and thus their responsibility—the apostles set about to right the situation. They admitted a fire was smoldering and hurried to extinguish it before it became a conflagration of defiling bitterness. They wisely suffered the short-lived pain of coping with the grievance.

The archenemy of the Church, Satan, was taking double aim at the infant fellowship, not only creating dissension, but trying to sidetrack the leaders from their main ministry. The apostles had been called to prayer and the ministry of God's Word, but along the way had been added the ministry of distributing alms to the needy. Recognizing that they were not fulfilling the new obligation, they must have been tempted to devote more time to this problem. But with divine insight they resisted the temptation, asserting it would be a serious mistake for them to neglect the Word of God to wait on tables (6:2). They would get help.

Alms distribution was a sacred service just as prayer and preaching. One ministered the living Bread, the other material bread; one by speaking, the other by supervising. Does not the harmonious working of a church depend on wise apportionment of its functions, just as the body operates smoothly when each of its parts performs its God-given task?

Involving the Congregation

Regardless of a church's form of government, it is wise to involve the entire membership in certain decisions. The apostles, after some preliminary thinking on the problem, convened the community of believers to invite the help of all. To the assembled disciples the apostles proposed their plan, then said: "Select from among you, brethren, seven men . . . whom we may put in charge of this task" (6:3, NASB).

Though the apostles suggested the solution, the entire congregation accepted the plan (6:5). The verse also notes that the congregation chose seven helpers, then presented them to the apostles. Here democracy, not clerical dictatorships, was part of the solution.

At the suggestion of the apostles, seven servants, or deacons, were chosen. Why seven? Many answers have been suggested. Because every Jewish village or town was presided over by seven leaders. Or because there were seven days in the week, one day for each deacon. Or because there were perhaps seven churches in Jerusalem, or districts, with each having one representative. Or because the number of converts now approached 7,000. Or because seven is a frequent and favorite number in Judaism throughout Scripture.

Though the number seven is not a pattern to be necessarily followed in present-day church government, the qualifications of these deacons are worthy of emulation. They were chosen not because they were somebody's relative or friend, or were successful or rich or personable, but because they measured up to a four-fold criterion of fitness. The apostles asked the congregation to select:

(1) believers—"among you"
(2) reputable—"of good reputation"
(3) Spirit-controlled—"full of the Spirit"
(4) wise—"full. . .of wisdom" (6:3, NASB).

The humble duties of table-serving—amazingly—called for sterling Christian graces plus sanctified common sense, enabling deacons to administer tactfully and lovingly in the delicate situation.

Going the Second Mile

A significant factor in the solution is indicated by the names of the chosen deacons: all seven bear Hellenistic names. Though some Hebrew Jews did have Greek names, the likelihood is that these men were all deliberately selected from the Hellenistic group.

The Hebrew majority could have officiously insisted, "We won't let those Greeks put anything over on us. We deserve a larger representation and the authority to see that things are done right." But here was a generous act of peacemaking by which the Hebrews said, "You think your widows are being neglected; then choose Grecian men to distribute the daily food. We're trusting the entire operation to you."

This policy has been followed outside church affairs. William Penn insisted in his colony that court cases involving Indians would have red men make up at least half of the jury.

And many churches have adopted conciliatory measures when a minority was grieved. In one disagreement between church youth and the decision-making adults over the time and rooms for a summer youth program, the official board appointed a committee with more young members than adults to work out the matter. The grateful youth responded with unexpected consideration for the adults.

In a church where the board of elders and board of deacons had frequent squabbles, the question of paying expenses for staff members to attend conventions threatened to add more fuel to the fire. Though they thought the matter was within their own authority, the elders respected the deacons' involvement in finances by referring the matter to a joint board. In good faith they approved a majority of deacons on the mediating board.

The "soft answer" by the Hebrews turned away the incipient wrath of the Hellenists. Their action said, "We need each other. We'll bear each others' burdens." Love overcame. Hebrew and Greek bowed their heads as the apostles led in prayer and laid hands of dedication on the seven deacons. The fellowship's first serious friction was beautifully mended, and ended.

Capitalizing on Crisis

Dissension need not bring disaster, but may bring delightful dividends as in this case.

Satan was unable to wedge in and split this church. The congregation's extremity became God's opportunity. As outsiders observed this fusion of desires, they were convinced of the reality of Christ. Had not Jesus said, "By this shall all men know that ye are my disciples"? (John 13:35) Wearing the badge of love so genuinely led to a harvest of souls: "And the Word of God increased, and the number of disciples multiplied in Jerusalem and a great company of the priests were obedient to the faith" (Acts 6:7).

Reports had circulated for some time about the miracles of a man called Jesus. As far back as the birth of John the Baptist, priests had heard that Zacharias' son would be the forerunner of the Messiah. In the last three years, priests had reported many cleansed lepers coming to offer a sacrifice after healing by the Galilean. And very recently the priests on duty when Jesus died recounted the ripping of the thick temple curtain from top to bottom, a feat no human could have performed. Many wondering about His messiahship were drawn into the fold of faith by the love of the believers in action.

Extending our view through the rest of Acts, we find that this first quarrel, righteously resolved, united the believers for a powerful proclamation of the Gospel in succeeding days of trial. Out of misunderstanding flowed missions of love to a spiritually hungry empire.

It happened this way:

Out of complaint came the election of seven deacons.

One of the deacons was Stephen. "Stephen, full of faith and power, did great wonders and miracles among the people" (6:8). Then Stephen was stoned to death.

But out of Stephen's martyrdom came the scattering of the Jerusalem saints through Judea and Samaria, and the conversion of Saul the zealous Hebrew who was goaded into surrender to Christ by the memory of Stephen's dying words (8:1-4; 9:5).

And out of Saul's conversion and commissioning came the evangelizing of the Roman empire.

Oddly, this expansion of the Gospel to the Gentile world precipitated the next recorded quarrel in the early Church, a controversy so serious it led to a major confrontation known as the First Church Council.

Robert Coote, writing in *Evangelical Newsletter* (Sept. 26, 1975) about the problem of racially integrated churches, describes four models and comments: "It is not easy to get to the heart of racism with a real cure, but a documented illustration may help.

"Some years ago a minority group with a Christian community felt cheated. The problem involved the equitable distribution of resources and the treating of the minority with respect and affirmation. The solution would determine whether the minority would be made to feel part of the group, whether they would be truly integrated.

"The leaders of the majority came up with a plan. Several

responsible men from the minority party were selected, and the money and resources were put in their hands. Henceforth the indigenous leaders of the minority handled the financial responsibility for the entire group, majority and minority alike.

"One of the seven became the first Christian martyr in that city. Another became the first Christian evangelist. The beautiful, direct, and simple solution in which they figured is documented in Acts 6."

3

Changing Culture or Timeless Truth?

A marble slab in a New Hampshire cemetery gives a wife's name, followed by this bitter, almost unbelievable epitaph: "Murdered by the Baptist Ministry and Churches." Then it proceeds to sketch the story. Apparently a pastor and a deacon had accused the woman of lying in a church meeting. She was condemned unheard, and reduced to poverty. When an exparte council was asked of the church, the latter voted not to receive any communication on the matter. The malicious assassination of the woman's character helped bring an early death. Her last words were, "Tell the truth and this iniquity will out."

The refusal of this church to discuss the matter contrasts vividly with the willingness of the early church at Jerusalem to listen to a delegation from the church at Antioch. The problem there was already disruptive and potentially explosive.

A Chronic Contention

Today people react with surprise to learn of a Jewish member or two within a local church, but the situation was reversed for the first decade of the Church. From the beginning, Jewish believers found it difficult to accept Gentile converts, even though the Great Commission specifically included "all nations" (Matt.

28:19). Peter had to be prepared by a heaven-sent vision to accept an invitation to preach to non-Jews at Caesarea. When he returned from his mission to the Roman soldier, Cornelius, the church leaders at Jerusalem called him to account. At first sharply critical, they finally accepted his explanation (Acts 11:18).

When Gentiles at Antioch in Syria began to join the new Hebrew-Christian church there, the surprised Jerusalem church sent Barnabas to investigate. So many more Gentiles believed on Christ that Barnabas sought Paul's help to instruct them. Later, sent out by this largely Gentile church to evangelize Asia Minor, Barnabas and Paul won hundreds more to Christ. When reports of the influx reached the Jerusalem church, some Jews found it difficult to accept Gentiles as spiritual equals. They revered Moses' laws and expected Christianity to retain its Old Testament heritage.

Up at Antioch there was no disharmony till Judaizing teachers from Jerusalem arrived and insisted on the necessity of the Jewish rite of circumcision for salvation (Acts 15:1). Providentially, Paul and Barnabas were back from their first missionary journey, and they resisted this bondage to legalism.

It's the Law!

The issue was critical. Either a person was saved by faith alone, or by faith together with meritorious works. If the latter, the Gospel of grace was virtually revoked. Paul and Barnabas recognized this as a battle for Christian liberty, the very crux of the Reformation church struggle to be fought 15 centuries later in Germany. There Luther's text from Romans, "The just shall live by faith" (1:17), ruled out the addition of penances, indulgences, priestly intercession, or human deeds of any kind as a basis for acceptance by God.

Paul and Barnabas had seen countless Gentiles won to Christ apart from Mosaic lawkeeping. With the missionary movement expected to penetrate farther into Gentile territory, this heresy would have to be handled. No doctrinal controversy could be more serious.

Seeking advice from the larger fellowship of believers on an overwhelming problem is a sign of strength, not weakness. Churches of like precious faith associate today for many purposes. Usually the goal is promotion of God's program, though occasionally it is opposition to Satan's advances.

In the summer of 1975, a group of Christian leaders met in a Minneapolis hotel to consider what the *New York Times* called the first major controversy to strike the charismatic movement. The center of contention was an alleged network of disciples linked by doctrine and loyalty in hierarchical fashion to a Florida-based organization. Leaders of the organization stress the need to disciple converts to maturity, but opponents claim the methods promote doctrinal and financial control. It is commendable, as in the Antiochan-Jerusalem conference, that consultation proceeded with sincere concern and without hostility.

Unable to appease the Judaizers from Jerusalem, the church at Antioch appointed Paul, Barnabas, and some other leaders to consult with the apostles and elders at Jerusalem about this dispute (Acts 15:2).

This meeting has been called the First Church Council, but theologian Frederic Farrar rejected that title. Bible teacher G. Campbell Morgan commented:

"He showed that the council at Jerusalem was not a convention of delegates, but a meeting of the church at Jerusalem to receive a deputation from the church at Antioch, and to consider a subject of grave importance in the matter of missionary enterprise. He pointed out, moreover, that this gathering in Jerusalem was for purposes of consultation, and not for final and dogmatic decision. Almost all councils subsequent to the first have attempted to fix some habit of ritual, or to give final form to the expression of some great truth. Neither of these things was attempted in the gathering in Jerusalem'' *(The Acts of the Apostles*, Fleming H. Revell, 1924, p. 355).

Why go to Jerusalem? Wasn't Antioch a close second to the mother church both in numbers and influence? Might not this conference degenerate into a battle between a Gentile church and a Jewish church? Paul and Barnabas were sent because an Antioch-Jerusalem coalition was sought on this crucial issue.

Since Jerusalem had first heard the Gospel, its real genius should be understood by Christians there. Also, since the apostles there could speak most authoritatively about the true Gospel, no higher council could be appealed to. And as Jerusalem was both the source and the stronghold of the error, vindication there of Paul's teaching would purify the stream of Christian proclamation.

A Solemn Assembly

Arriving at Jerusalem, they were welcomed by the church, the apostles, and the elders. The missionary team reported God's marvelous deeds through them, doubtless highlighting the conversions of Gentiles. But some Christian Pharisees objected and said in effect, ''Go back and tell those Gentiles that if they want full admission into the church they must submit to the law of Moses and the covenant of circumcision.''

Sensing the importance of the dispute, the apostles and elders called a special meeting of the church.

More mature and rocklike than in his younger days, Peter kept silent as the debate went back and forth. Then he rose and said that God decided the question some time back when Cornelius' family had been saved by faith and given the Holy Spirit just as had happened to the believing Jews. Why tempt God, asked Peter, by adding on Gentile shoulders a yoke even Jewish forefathers found an impossible burden? There is but one way—''through grace''—for both Jew and Gentile (vv. 7-11).

So strong was the impact of Peter's words that silence reigned. Barnabas spoke next, before Paul, because Barnabas had been well-known in Jerusalem long before Paul's conversion. They added their testimony to Peter's about God's redeeming quest among the Gentiles (v. 12).

Again there was quiet, so convincing were the combined witnesses. Then the chairman, James, spoke. Apparently the leader of the church, he supported Peter's testimony, then pointed out that Gentile response to the Gospel fulfilled Old Testament prophecy, and had been God's plan from "long ago." Then he gave his judgment: "We should not make it difficult for the Gentiles who are turning to God" (v. 19, NIV).

James is sometimes accused of contradicting Paul on the relation of works to faith because of his epistle emphasizing works (James 2:17, 20, 24, 26). But, at the Jerusalem conference, James and Paul agree completely that works are not necessary for salvation.

It is instructive that the verdict of the council was not decided by a vote of the participants. Facts are facts regardless of people's opinions, and the apostles knew the facts. Some children watching a calf frisking around a field argued whether it was a "boy calf or a girl calf." Finally one child piped up, "I know how we can tell: let's vote on it." But the truth of animal gender or doctrinal reality is not decided by poll-taking. Paul would have rejected any decision at that conference that denied the Gospel of grace revealed to him by Christ, as he emphasized in the epistle to the Galatian church (Gal. 1:6-9).

Similarly, any church conclave today which downgrades a fundamental doctrine transmitted by the apostles through their writings must be repudiated by loyal followers of Christ. No church council can add to, subtract from, or change in any way divine truth as revealed in the Scriptures.

Firmness and Flexibility

To his verdict, James added his recommendations for Gentile believers' conduct that would conciliate Jewish believers who found it hard to comprehend "freedom from the law." Gentile

Christians were admonished to abstain from certain practices forbidden to Old Testament Jews. These concessions would enhance fellowship, ease suspicious fears of the Jewish community, and cement peace among the brethren. In later decades the ritualistic scruples would become less relevant.

James' compromise was paralleled later by Paul's principle of surrendering certain liberties that would mislead a weaker brother. Both were loving measures prescribed for the good of the whole church.

A devout German couple drank beer and wine with their Christian friends in their homeland. After moving to the eastern U.S., they discovered their new Christian friends frowned on alcohol as a beverage, so the couple graciously surrendered their old practice. Their habit broke no law, but it wounded Christian love.

The "whole church" shared in the ratification and sending of representatives to Antioch (v. 22), and the entire church there gathered to hear the decision (v. 30). Judas Barsabas and Silas, both prophets from Jerusalem (vv. 22-23), accompanied the Antiochan delegation, and confirmed the authenticity of the letter summarizing the council's findings.

When the official letter was read, the people were delighted (v. 31). What relief to have so vital a matter amicably settled and with the faith of the Gospel still intact. The two prophets from Jerusalem stayed a while to encourage the brethren—had there been no conflict, the Antiochan church would have missed their ministry! The two delegates returned to Jerusalem with the blessing of the Antioch church; never had the two churches been so united.

Doubtless Paul would have preferred to spend his efforts in church-planting than in disputing with fellow Christians, but the desirable had to be sacrificed to unpleasant necessity in order to maintain the truth of the Gospel. Decisiveness and devotion had overcome a major obstacle in Paul's mission to the ends of the empire. With full backing by the Jerusalem church, he could proclaim the liberating news: "A man is justified by faith without the deeds of the law" (Rom. 3:28).

After the partnership of Paul and Barnabas ended, Paul chose Silas as his co-worker. A more propitious choice could not have been made. Wherever they went, Paul's message of forgiveness through faith was seconded by Silas, a leader from the Jewish-oriented Jerusalem church. And together they delivered the verdict reached by the Jerusalem council to churches along the way (Acts 16:4-5).

The Jew-Gentile issue has surfaced in recent times in different form. Many Jewish believers today want to retain enriching Jewish distinctives. The spreading Christian Messianic movement in the U.S. is inclined toward calling meeting places synagogues and its ministers rabbis, conducting services Friday night, using Jewish terms like "Yeshua" instead of "Jesus," celebrating Jewish holidays, and in some cases wanting to be known as the fourth branch of Judaism (with Orthodox, Conservative, and Reform). This emphasis on Jewishness caused the 60-year-old Hebrew Christian Alliance of America to change its name to the Messianic Jewish Alliance. The purpose is to gain a wider hearing of the Gospel and its already-come Messiah.

Without question, no Jewish practice or rite should be added to faith as essential for salvation. On the other hand, wise concessions can be made for a more palatable and understandable witness to the Jewish community. If talented Jewish music groups can catch the ear of spiritually alienated Jews and teach Gentile congregations to sing Messiah's hallelujahs with Eastern tempo, perhaps a new day for Jewish missions is around the corner.

When the leadership of the Holy Spirit is followed, calm supplants storm and blessing banishes battle. The official letter of the first inter-church conference put it, "It seemed good to the Holy [Spirit] and to us" (Acts 15:28). G. Campbell Morgan commented:

"We must freely admit we very seldom hear this language. We

do read that a matter was carried by an overwhelming majority, but that is a very different thing. An overwhelming majority often leaves behind it a minority disaffected and dangerous. We shall come to unanimity when we are prepared to discuss freely, frankly our absolute differences, on the basis of a common desire to know the mind of the Lord. If we come . . .having made our minds up that so it must be, then we hinder the Holy Spirit, and make it impossible for Him to make known His mind and will. But if we come, perfectly sure in our minds, but wanting to know what the Lord's mind is, then ere the council ends, today as yesterday, the moment will come when we shall be able to say with a fine dignity and a splendid force, 'It seems good to the Holy Spirit and to us' " (*The Acts of the Apostles*, p. 365).

4

When Co-Workers Clash

The director of evangelism for the Navigators organization, LeRoy Eims, tells about a recruit, Johnny, joining his evangelistic team during LeRoy's first year in Christian service. Things went well for several months, with Johnny dedicated and enthusiastic. Then one weekend Johnny failed to arrive for team witnessing on the Iowa State University campus. He had simply decided not to come. The following Monday Eims informed Johnny that he was no longer on the team because he had broken one of the standards of the group. Johnny took it hard.

Two weeks later Eims got a letter from Johnny, thanking him for making it mean something to be part of the team, then listing 13 reasons why he should be reaccepted. Eims immediately welcomed him back, and Johnny became one of the most productive men on the team. In later years he served the Lord on two continents. Writes Eims, "As I look back over a 20-year perspective, I know I would handle the situation differently today. I would be quicker to show the tenderness and gentleness of Christ. But the principle remains inviolate" (*Be the Leader You Were Meant to Be,* Victor Books, © 1975, pp. 62-63).

Some 1900 years ago Paul and Barnabas had a similar falling-out. Their young assistant, John Mark, had a spiritual lapse, and

Paul was inclined to be tough while Barnabas preferred to be tender. The sharp, unresolved contention caused a split between these spiritual giants. The episode affords insights in understanding and resolving conflicts between Christian brethren today.

Godly Men May Have Opposing Views

Paul and Barnabas, two of the best-known New Testament leaders, both called apostles, and close co-workers in pastoral and missionary ministries, found themselves at odds over the best way to do the Lord's work. In fact, so firm were their convictions and so fierce their contention that they went their separate ways.

This painful separation shows the humanity of these apostles, men of limited wisdom and imperfect character. Never should we set human beings on a pedestal, or expect one to compare with Jesus. Early church leaders were not stained-glass characters, but flesh-and-blood mortals who had quarrels which could lead to hot temper and consequent coolness. Their failures do not undermine their overall ministry, but they remind us that God uses fallible people to do His sacred work.

Through the centuries sincere Christian people have stood on opposite sides of many issues. What is vital in every disagreement is openness to God's leading and love for the disputant. Christians who disagree honestly and peaceably can still serve God honorably.

Each Side May Be Valid

After the Jerusalem church council, Paul suggested he and Barnabas visit the churches they had established on their first missionary journey. Barnabas agreed, adding that he wanted to take Mark along. That name raised a red flag before Paul because Mark had abandoned the team when he was needed in Asia Minor (Acts 13:5, 13). The suitability or pseudo-ability of Mark for further ministry was the bone of contention.

Why did Mark defect? Did he return to Jerusalem because he

was homesick? Was his mother, likely a widow, somewhat dependent on him? Or did Mark resent Paul taking over the leadership from his cousin Barnabas? Mention of Mark's defection is found in the sentence which gives the first indication of Paul's primacy on the team (v. 13). Or, as they branched out to strong Gentile territory in Asia Minor, was Mark, close friend of apostle-to-the-Jews Peter, not yet sympathetic with Paul's readiness to preach the Gospel to the Gentiles? Or was Mark afraid of what was ahead—rugged, robber-infested country, unfriendly reception, even persecution? Had his youthfulness gotten the better of him, showing that he was just not yet ready for rigorous missionary activity, perhaps running ahead of God's will for his life?

Paul and Barnabas did what countless Christians have done through the centuries right up to recent committee, board, or business meetings in churches around the world. Let's imagine their possible dialogue.

Paul: Mark? We can't take him. He failed us last time.

Barnabas: But that was last time.

Paul: He's likely to fail us again. He's a deserter.

Barnabas: He's had time to think it over. We've got to give him another chance. He's got the makings of a missionary.

Paul: Tell me, Barnabas, isn't it because he's your cousin that you want to take him again?

Barnabas: That's not fair. You know I've tried to help many people who aren't my relatives. I'm convinced this lad needs understanding encouragement.

Paul: We need someone who can stand up to persecution, an angry mob, beatings, perhaps jail. Our team has to be close-knit, thoroughly reliable. How can we trust a lad who failed like Mark? No, Barnabas. Recall the words of the Master: "No man who puts his hand to the plow, and looks back, is fit for the kingdom of God."

Barnabas: I've talked with him about his failure. I'm sure he won't defect again. To refuse him might do spiritual damage at the moment of his repentance. It'd be like breaking a bruised reed, like quenching smoking flax.

Each had a strong argument. Paul thought the *ministry* to eternal souls would be jeopardized by softness to Mark. Barnabas deemed that the *man*, a potential disciple, would be endangered by severity.

How often the same type of conflict surfaces in church life: the ministry versus the man, the work versus the worker, the principle versus the person. A Sunday School teacher is needed for a high school class When a name is suggested, some object because he is too new a Christian, and could harm the students' development. But others point out he has matured much since his conversion and would grow considerably through this assignment. Partisans take sides, sometimes with ill feelings.

Seeking Wise Compromise

Members of one growing church confessed, "Sure, we've had disagreements about the size of the pulpit, the order of service, choice of staff members, and some very serious matters, but still we don't lose control and disrupt the Lord's work. Always some folks concede a little to help reach a satisfactory decision."

Could Paul or Barnabas, or both, have developed a reasonable compromise? Giving in would not have meant heresy, for no doctrine was involved. Could Paul have said: "We'll tell him he's on probation; if he doesn't work out the first month, we'll send him home again."

Or perhaps Barnabas could have conceded: "We do need dedicated workers on our team; let's give Mark a minor assignment to see how he does. Meanwhile we'll start on our journey, and if we hear he's measuring up, we'll send for him to join us along the way."

Or could they have agreed on a contingent plan? "Let's take Mark, but also others. If Mark deserts us again, we'll have others to fall back on."

Going back to the new Christian suggested for the Sunday School class, a compromise solution could let the candidate substitute-teach or take a helping role. Evaluation of his performance would give both sides a better basis for a decision.

A growing church which attracted a wide spectrum of believers disagreed over the kind of worship for the Sunday morning service. Guitar music, folk tunes, and talk-back sermons were creeping into what had been a rather dignified affair. The old-timers wanted the formal service restored; polarization was developing. The two groups met to seek the Spirit's wisdom and happily accepted a proposal to devote the evening service to contemporary worship forms, returning the morning hour to the traditional style. A prayerful and loving spirit helped bring a satisfying solution for both parties.

Paul was endorsed by the church at Antioch as he left with his new partner Silas, but such endorsement for Barnabas is not mentioned (15:40). Some Bible readers have concluded the church took Paul's side in the dispute, but the report may only indicate that the record from here on focuses on Paul. The argument from silence is not impressive in this case.

Keeping Their Cool in the Furnace

The main part of the Greek word used to describe the apostles' contention means "sharp." In its compound form it gives us our English paroxysm. The Septuagint used this word to describe the great indignation which led God to root Israel out of its land (Deut. 29:28). Doctor Luke, the author of the report in Acts, well knew that this medical word was used of a sudden seizure, spasm, or the point at which a disease took a turn for the worse, breaking forth in its severest form. The altercation between Paul and Barnabas broke into acute, fierce form. Personal feelings ran high.

Discussion and disagreement are inevitable, but losing one's "cool" is wrong. In beginning to raise one's voice, one has to be careful that he's making a point of argument, not manifesting anger or contempt. A sign of spiritual as well as emotional maturity is the ability to argue without losing self-control. "The wrath of man worketh not the righteousness of God" (James 1:20).

Separation May Be Best

Since each insisted on his own way, Paul and Barnabas parted company, ending their partnership of many years. Barnabas went first, sailing with Mark to Cyprus. Paul headed into Asia Minor with Silas to strengthen the churches (Acts 15:22, 39-41).

When two strong persons or factions find themselves diametrically opposed, the best solution may be to separate so each can wholeheartedly pursue its own objective. An unresolvable difference is often best served by amicable, sensitive sundering.

Church history records numerous divisions between leaders, churches, and organizations, some rancid and jarring, others sweet and gentle. Innumerable Christians have severed associations on good terms in order to take up a different kind of ministry incompatible with their former pattern but conformed to God's plan.

God Can Bless Division

Though the friction between Paul and Barnabas was unpleasant and regrettable, their break-up proved productive, bringing blessing in disguise. Because God can make angry men praise Him, divine providence can override a division to yield compensating dividends. Contrary to the ecumenical thesis for church union, a division of forces may further the Lord's work.

With two Gospel teams, Barnabas-Mark and Paul-Silas, the work was extended so that more churches were founded and more souls won. Church-growth leader C. Peter Wagner points out that clashes between dynamic new leaders and settled older pastors in Latin American churches have resulted in what has been termed "growth by splitting." Says Wagner, "No one will say that church splits are intrinsically good. They frequently involve nasty quarrels and legal hassles. Often they leave broken hearts and permanent enemies behind. Nevertheless, God promises that all things work together for good to them that love God (Rom. 8:28). Strangely enough, church splits among Pentecostals have frequently resulted in accelerated growth for both sides of the split'' (*Look Out, the Pentecostals Are Coming,* Creation House, p. 62).

Countless churches have been born through splits. Dozens of denominations likewise issued from irreconcilable contention. Many Christian organizations developed out of strong disagreement between leaders, some spurred by important principles and others by fractious personalities.

Does this endorse ecclesiastical altercations in order to multiply churches, missionary societies, and Christian organizations? A thousand times—no! The peace of a church and of a Christian organization is very important. Church or Christian organization splits bring disrepute to Christ's cause and sometimes disaster to the participants. Only God's grace, in union or division, produces progress.

The two teams headed for different localities, perhaps as a conciliatory move, or a first-century harmonious arrangement. Barnabas and Mark sailed to the island of Cyprus. Paul and Silas moved to Asia Minor, aiming at the continent. At least they didn't start churches in each other's backyard, as some splitting congregations have been known to do in our day.

At first, both likely suffered embarrassing moments when old friends on Cyprus asked Barnabas, ''Where's Paul?'' and in Asia Minor asked Paul, ''How come Barnabas isn't with you?'' Barnabas, so warm toward people, and Paul, who wrote ''the greatest of these is love,'' would reach out toward each other. A few years later Paul referred kindly to Barnabas in one of his letters (1 Cor. 9:6). Though they did not resume their partnership, the sharp contention did yield to the gentle persuasion of love as they kept up on each other's ministry, their paths perhaps crossing on occasion.

John Wesley and George Whitefield were good friends in their earlier years, Wesley having begun his outdoor preaching ministry at Whitefield's encouragement. As time went on the men disagreed, with Whitefield leaning more heavily toward Calvinism than his younger friend's Arminianism. When Whitefield died, Wesley was asked if he expected to see Dr. Whitefield in heaven. In exaggerated but honest respect he answered, "No, he'll be so near the throne of God that men like me will never even get a glimpse of him!" Though differing, they did not lose their sense of oneness in Christ.

Casualty Reclaimed

One significant outcome was that Mark made good. From his first imprisonment at Rome, Paul wrote of Mark as a fellow-worker (Phile. 24) and a comfort to him (Col. 4:10-11). To earn such commendation, Mark must have spent some time along the way serving with Paul. In his last recorded epistle, written from a Roman dungeon, Paul asked that Mark be sent to him, "because he is helpful to me in my ministry" (2 Tim. 4:11, NIV). In his final days Paul wanted one whom he had rejected in his earlier years.

Mark traveled widely preaching the Gospel. Tradition says he evangelized in Egypt and North Africa. St. Mark's Square in Venice is named for him. And the same Mark gave us the Gospel of the perfect Servant, the Lord Jesus Christ.

He who failed at first as a servant wrote about the unfailing Supreme Servant in the second book of the New Testament. Both Paul's sternness and Barnabas' tenderness may have contributed to this great blessing to the church.

5

A Fight Over Spirituality

The *Police Gazette* was never noted for reverence, and the editors must have chortled over a church-related item printed in a bygone era. It seems that a Tennessee belle wore a crinoline to church—the first time anyone in town had worn the wide and unwieldy hoopskirt. It received much comment from the parishioners, not all favorable. Some thought the outfit a dangerous eccentricity, even unchristian. When a deacon tripped over—or kicked—her skirt, a riot broke out. Fellow worshipers mixed it up, punching, kicking, and scratching, according to the wide-eyed reporter.

More than one church dispute has flared over whether certain cultural practices should be allowed. The early church at Rome had such a problem, and though it seems trivial or ridiculous to us today, it involved an important principle and pushed the church toward a serious rift.

The Issue

Most of the Roman populace, except for the Jews and the Christians, worshiped idols. Banquets, birthdays, and other celebrations often served meat that was dedicated to idols in the temples before transfer to the markets for public sale. Converted Jews, full of scruples for the Mosaic code of permitted food and full of loathing for idols, insisted that Christians could have nothing to do with such meat—even though it often was of highest quality.

These people were not like the Judaizers who made salvation dependent on something added to faith, else Paul would have rebuked them severely. But their "weak" conscience caused them to continue to observe Jewish dietary laws and sabbaths.

Most Gentile believers at Rome were rejoicing in their Christ-given liberation. They rejected idol worship, but they did not see anything immoral in eating meat previously dedicated in the temples when they knew an idol was nothing but a piece of carved stone or wood. So they ate meat whenever they pleased, even at social events in the temple.

With these two groups holding opposite viewpoints, and each deeming itself more spiritual than the other, the stage was set for trouble. In his letter to the Roman church, Paul pinpointed the mutual censure and uncharitable judgment that had likely already strained the fellowship (Rom 14:1-3). Recognizing the rightness in each position, Paul rebukes both for their critical disparagement of the other.

Wide disagreements exist today in our churches over certain practices. A Christian from the South may be repelled by a swimming party for both men and women, then offend his Northern brother by lighting up a cigarette. At an international conclave for missionaries, a woman from the Orient could not wear sandals with a clear conscience. A Christian from western Canada thought it worldly for a Christian acquaintance to wear a wedding ring, and a woman from Europe thought it almost immoral for a wife not to wear a ring that signaled her status. A man from Denmark was pained to even watch British Bible school students play football, while the British students shrank from his pipe smoking.

Many a congregation, as preacher William Barclay puts it, has been "torn in two because those who hold broader and more liberal views are angrily contemptuous of those whom they regard as stick-in-the-mud, die-hard conservatives and puritans; and because those who are stricter in their outlook are critical, censorious, and condemning of those who wish the right to do things which they think are wrong" (*The Letter to the Romans*, Westminster Press, p. 199).

Conflict in the church at Rome had intensified to the point, conjectures one scholar, where "probably the church refused membership to those who held eccentric views," so Paul was seeking to avoid further schism.

Contention from this disagreement or another was still there a few years later when Paul arrived in Rome as a prisoner of the emperor. From his own hired house, Paul wrote in the Philippian letter that some Roman Christians were proclaiming Christ because of envy, strife, and contention (Phil. 1:15-16). The faction that insisted on observing Old Testament ceremonial laws—in direct contradiction to Paul's teaching—took advantage of his confinement to promote their viewpoint and distress Paul.

Unbelievable as it seems, fairly substantial evidence suggests that strife between these two groups was responsible for the martyrdom of many Roman Christians. Near the end of the first century a Christian leader in Rome, Clement, wrote a letter to the church in Corinth. His main thrust was to reprimand a spirit of envy and animosity in the Corinthian church. To show the dire consequences of such strife, Clement indicated that about the time of Paul's incarceration a vast number of believers had been martyred because of jealousy.

Theologian Oscar Cullmann, in his book *Peter*, concludes that these martyrs (and he includes Paul and Peter) were victims of jealous strife from persons who counted themselves members of the Christian church at Rome. Rivalry between factions at the capital became so bitter that some brethren handed in names of their Christian opponents as traitors to the empire. After sifting the evidence, Cullmann sadly concludes that envy among Christians helped feed saints to the lions in the coliseum and lit fires under Christian brethren in Nero's gardens. What terrible conflagrations can rise from spiteful sparks!

To Do or Not to Do

Paul classified the two factions at Rome as "the strong" and "the weak," or the convinced and the doubters. The wrong was plainly not in the controversial action, but in the injured consciences and the animosity that smothered love in the fellowship. Because each group was vulnerable to specific failings, Paul gave explicit instruction to both.

In many life situations the strong are tempted to disdain the weak. The boy who can run faster, throw farther, and lift more tends to scorn the one who cannot do as well. Spiritually strong people tend to look down on the weak, regarding them as ignorant, odd, or perverse. What the weak need is loving acceptance. "Accept the one who is weak in faith," Paul directed (Rom. 14:1, NASB).

Weak believers should be accepted readily into church membership. The church is not a museum for perfect people, but a school for the spiritually illiterate and a hospital for the spiritually ill. New and weak Christians should be welcomed for training in reliance on the Lord, not for indoctrination in a code of conduct.

Are you confident in your faith? Don't belittle or belabor the uncertain believer.

The command not to judge one another in debatable matters is strongly emphasized (Rom 14:4, 10-12). Why judge a person whom God has accepted? It is the Master's role to judge His servant—God's responsibility, not ours. Many acts and attitudes are obviously evil and clearly prohibited, but others become right or wrong according to the inner motivation.

Each person, confident or uncertain, must be fully persuaded in his own mind under the leadership of Christ. Since personalities, needs, and opportunities differ, our conclusions will vary on morally debatable practices. Theologian J. Gresham Machen counseled Christians to keep their consciences free from "the tyranny of experts." Not conformity to the crowd, but conviction of the heart should decide these questionable matters.

Does a custom or practice appear evil to you? Avoid it, and let other Christians answer to God, not to you.

But the confident-strong are not off Paul's hook yet. They can be wrong in doing a right action! For if their conduct induces an uncertain-weak Christian to do something he believes is wrong, they have injured their brother. Violations of one's conscience is moral failure and an obstacle in the path of spiritual progress. For the strong to recklessly disregard his brother's conscience is to destroy the work of God (v. 20). Rather, Paul advised, "follow after the things which make for peace and things wherewith one may edify another" (v. 19).

Knowledge puffs up, but love builds up. In the midst of a believing community, the viewpoint of other believers should be taken into consideration. Paul's words to the Roman Christians can fit many similar situations today: "Let us not judge one another any more, but rather determine this—not to put an obstacle or a stumbling block in a brother's way. . . . For if because of food your brother is hurt, you are no longer walking according to love. Do not destroy with your food him for whom Christ died. . . . It is good not to eat meat or to drink wine, or to do anything by which your brother stumbles" (vv. 13, 15, 21; NASB).

Church-growth leader C. Peter Wagner says, "Some Christians think that they should never patronize a commercial theater. Others think that they can, but that they should be selective with their movies just as they are with their literature. This is where relativity comes in, and decisions should be made on the principles of love and the weaker brother" *(A Turned-on Church in an Uptight World*, Zondervan Publishing House, 1971, p. 76).

Are you truly strong? Then bear with the burdens of the weak.

An eye-catching drawing in a magazine depicted a muscular

man holding a picture of himself before he developed his physique. The picture pointed up the title of an article, "Don't Be a 95-lb. Christian Weakling!" The article began by reminding us how often we have heard sermons on the responsibility of treating a weaker brother with love lest we lead him to fall. Though such advice is scriptural and needed, author William Coleman says, "The time has come to address the weaker brother: 'Why don't you grow up and stop being so easily offended?' " *(Eternity*, March 1975, p. 15)

Good point. If "the weaker brother" is a person who expects others to live by his scruples and becomes offended when they do not comply, his faith is feeble. Such faith confuses life-style with righteousness—sports, television, fashions, and musical fads with humility, compassion, purity, and peaceableness.

Warmed by Love

Sixteenth-century theologian Melanchthon summed it up: "In essentials, unity; in non-essentials, liberty; in all things, charity."

Paul wrote, "For the kingdom of God is not meat and drink, but righteousness, and peace, and joy in the Holy [Spirit]" (v. 17). He could have added, "nor rings, nor cosmetics, nor clothes, nor guitars" and a host of other things not expressly handled in the Scriptures. Neither our standing before God nor inner peace is dependent upon matters of moral indifference.

An elderly lady in Massachusetts could not bear to see stray cats out in the cold winter night. One January evening she sheltered six stray cats plus her own dog and cat. After retiring she was suddenly stricken with an illness and could not get out of bed. The house grew cold as her stove fire died out. Windows rattled as the wind howled through the night. The temperature dropped to zero.

Neighbors found the woman the next day in her bed, warm as toast. On each side of her head purred a stray cat. Another was draped like a fur piece around her neck. Two were snuggled under her armpits and two more against her sides. Her dog lay across her stomach. The strays she had befriended had saved her life.

The church should also harbor the straying, the misfits, the sick. Welcomed and nourished, they could protect the church from a slow freeze into professionalism and formalism. The "weak" need care, but they are alive and they give new warmth to the body.

6

Following the Real Leader

A news story from Wales told of a feud in a church looking for a new pastor. It read:

"Yesterday the two opposition groups both sent ministers to the pulpit. Both spoke simultaneously, each trying to shout above the other. Both called for hymns, and the congregation sang two—each side trying to drown out the other. Then the groups began shouting at each other. Bibles were raised in anger. The Sunday morning service turned into a bedlam. Through it all, the two preachers continued to outshout each other with their sermons.

"Eventually a deacon called a policeman. Two came in and began shouting for the congregation to be quiet. They advised the 40 persons in the church to return home. The rivals filed out, still arguing. Last night one of the group called a 'let's-be-friends' meeting. It broke up in argument."

The item was headlined, "Hallelujah! Two Jacks in One Pulpit." It could have been bannered, "Two Factions in One Fellowship."

In the Corinthian fellowship there were four factions. Paul begins his letter to this church: "Now I beseech you, brethren, by the name of our Lord Jesus Christ, that ye all speak the same thing, and that there be no divisions among you; but that ye be perfectly joined together in the same mind and in the same judgment'' (1 Cor. 1:10).

The next verse speaks of ''quarreling'' (NASB), a word elsewhere translated ''strife'' (Gal. 5:20), and a much harsher word than the ''divisions'' of 1 Corinthians 1:10. A division or schism may form without creating nasty feelings, but a contentious quarrel suggests expression of animosity. The church was split into four factions.

The same situation has recurred over and over through the years. Someone penned this parody of ''Win Them One by One.''

''You split the one next to you,
And I'll split the one next to me;
In no time at all,
We'll split them all,
So split them, split them, one by one.''

Paul wrote to the Corinthians about five years after starting the church there. Word reached him in Ephesus of several problems in the Corinthian church, and he responded with this letter which has been called the outstanding textbook on pastoral theology. The major problem was division in the church body, reported by a source Paul is careful to mention.

Too often information is passed along like this: ''Pastor, did you know that so-and-so is doing this—but don't let him know I told you.'' Or an anonymous letter arrives: ''Dear Deacon, Mr. X is a hypocrite. I hope you discipline him. From a faithful follower of Christ.''

One pastor on receiving a phone call with such information replies, ''I'll be glad to take that up with the party if I can use your name.'' Almost always the caller expresses horror at the thought of personal implication. But not Paul's informants. Chloe and her household were quite willing to speak up and be identified.

The verb translated, "hath been declared" means "made evident or clear"; Paul writes what he knows to be true. And the information came to him personally; he is not reacting to a rumor, nor was he relying on a single witness.

In a Canadian church with a succession of three pastors in ten years, some old-timers often expressed a preference for Pastor A. "He got along with everyone so well," they reminisced. Others claimed Pastor B as their favorite: "What a pulpiteer!" Still others lauded Pastor C: "He was such a great visitor." Others, of course, praised the present pastor, revealing wide discontent in the church.

Choosing Sides

Believers were similarly divided at Corinth. They formed cliques around four names. Some lined up behind Paul, saying, "I follow Paul." Others bragged, "I support Apollos." Others clamored: "I revere Peter." The super-spiritual—or genuinely wise—declared: "I am of Christ" (v. 12).

Experts in interpersonal relationships tell us that when people line up consistently on one side and others on a second, the differences are destructive. But if Mr. A finds himself voting with Mr. B on some issues as well as occasionally against him, polarization of positions is avoided. At Corinth the same people lined up inflexibly on the same side.

Since Paul was the founder of the church, many would make him preeminent, especially those converted under his ministry. Proud of their association with him from the beginning, they looked on successors as rivals. When later preachers came, these people quickly noted differences from Paul and enlarged the halo around the apostle's head. Traditionalists to the core, they probably lamented the passing of "the good old days." The status quo was enshrined.

Apollos, who came to Corinth after Paul left, was an eloquent preacher and "mighty in the Scriptures" (Acts 18:24). Perhaps with his brilliance and Alexandrian background, he tried to relate Christianity to philosophy. "He can certainly sway an audience," some marveled. Apollos did not encourage this excessive admiration. In fact, his unwillingness to widen this split at Corinth may have delayed his return (1 Cor. 16:12).

Though Cephas (Peter) probably had not yet visited Corinth, he had a loyal following there. Known as the apostle to the Jews, he would attract those who believed in observing the Mosaic law. Well known as number one of the twelve disciples, he would be ranked far ahead of the Johnny-come-latelies Paul and Apollos.

The fourth faction said, "We follow no human leader. And we go back farther than even Peter. We go back to Christ." Perhaps some had seen Christ in the flesh or based their creed on some portion of His teaching.

But by their affirmation of Christ, this group may have proudly implied that all others did not belong to Christ as they did, relegating them to second-class believers.

Paul had no objections to legitimate honors given to other preachers. But he knew that exalting any man unduly would erect a fence around him and create an exclusiveness that dishonored the name of Christ, with a theme song like this:

> Believe as I believe, no more, no less;
> That I am right, and no one else, confess;
> Feel as I feel, think only as I think;
> Eat what I eat, and drink but what I drink;
> Look as I look, do always as I do;
> And then, and only then, I'll fellowship with you.
>
> (source unknown)

The Corinthian cliques have their successors down through the centuries. Some groups claim to preach the simple Gospel; others the Gospel with the full complement of points. Some idealize a system of theology; others exult in liturgy and ritual; still others hold high "the Bible and the Bible alone." Ever present is the danger of looking down on others whose emphasis varies.

Some jokesters tell about the three churches standing at the same intersection. One congregation could be heard singing, "Will there be any stars in my crown?" followed by the second's: "No, not one," and the third's triumphant: "Oh, that will be glory for me."

A group of theologians were discussing predestination and free will. When the argument became heated the dissidents split into two groups. One man, unable to make up his mind which group to join, slipped into the predestination crowd. Challenged as to why he was there, he said, "I came of my own free will." The group retorted: "Free will? You can't join us!" He retreated to the opposing group and met the same challenge. "I was sent here," he answered honestly. "Get out!" they stormed. "You can't join us unless you come of your own free will." And the confused Christian was out in the cold.

Charles Wesley wrote some of his hymns to promote Brother John's doctrine of "entire sanctification." The second verse of his "Love Divine, All Loves Excelling" asks God to "take away our bent to sinning." Some Calvinists rejected the song as teaching an unbiblical perfectionism.

A divisive issue among evangelicals in Dwight Moody's day was eschatology, the doctrine of the future. Postmillenarian teaching was giving way to premillenarian interpretation. In the 1890s the premillenialists began to dispute among themselves, and Moody advised them: "Don't criticize if our watches don't agree about the time we know He is coming."

Paul rebukes the jealousy and division occasioned by human exaltation. Had a fundamental doctrine been the issue, Paul would have taken sides. None of the cliques held heretical views; the error on the resurrection, treated in chapter 15, seems to have been a general misconception held by all the groups.

As long as our knowledge is imperfect and our preferences vary, Christians will disagree on doctrinal emphases, organizational structure, and liturgical matters, perpetuating denominational divisions. Such proliferation may contribute to the vigor and devoutness of Christianity as a whole. Paul does not rebuke denominations fostered by conscientious conviction, but fragments wrenched from the whole body by contentious, conceited people.

Diversity does not require division, but a divisive spirit promotes harmful division. Paul focused on the main issue by querying the Corinthians about Christ.

One Team

Paul asked three questions. First, "Is Christ divided?" The verb *divided* derives from a noun meaning "part." Has Christ been ripped into parts so that four cliques each had a quarter of Him? No group has an exclusive claim to Christ, nor can He be apportioned with others as co-Saviour or team leader. All of Christ is for every believer, and for every group of believers.

Each segment of Christians should try to learn from the emphasis of the other groups instead of haughtily withdrawing to its own corner. Remember the six blind men who were asked to describe an elephant after touching it? The one who touched its leg compared it to a tree. He who touched its side, a wall. Its ear was likened to a fan, its trunk a snake, its tusk a spear, and its tail a rope. Each man needed the input of the others to get a complete picture.

Truth is multifaceted. The Holy Spirit used four men, Matthew, Mark, Luke, and John, to give us a balanced picture of Jesus Christ as King, Servant, Man, and God. None of the Gospels is more faithful to Christ than the others. How foolish to build a wall around some section of truth and fail to see truth in other believing groups.

Paul then asks: "Was Paul crucified for you?" Did any of the preachers lauded by the Corinthians die on a cross to make atonement for sin? Disgust and sorrow must have choked Paul to think any clique at Corinth would bestow on any human the honor and trust due exclusively to the eternal Saviour who gave Himself for us.

Third question from Paul: "Were ye baptized in the name of Paul?" Baptism is administered in the name of Jesus Christ, which means identification with and submission to that divine person. None of the Corinthians had been baptized in the name of Paul, Apollos, or Peter.

Someone has suggested we should turn our denominational nouns into adjectives. Instead of saying, "I am a Baptist, Methodist, Calvinist, Arminian, charismatic, fundamentalist, etc.," we should designate ourselves as a Baptist Christian, a Methodist Christian," and so forth, to accent our *Christian* oneness. After meeting genuine believers of another persuasion, rather than commenting, "He baptizes by immersion," or "He speaks in tongues," we would say, "He's a Christian brother (or sister); we have claim on each other."

A white-haired man stood before a gallery painting of Christ. Face aglow, he murmured, "Bless Him; I love Him." A stranger overheard and said, "Brother, I love Him too," and clasped the old man's hand. A third man caught the word and joining his hand said, "I love Him too." Before the picture stood a group of people, hand clasped to hand, strangers but united in one Lord. They discovered they belonged to different denominations, but they belonged primarily to Christ. Putting Christ before human leaders will help fulfill Paul's wish "that there should be no schism in the body" (1 Cor. 12:25).

Just as we cheer a favorite athletic team, ancient Greeks supported their favorite philosopher in a sort of fan club. This worldly practice had crept into the Corinthian church so that people lined up behind their favorite wisdom dispenser; the erudite Paul, the eloquent Apollos, or the chief-disciple Peter. Because the Corinthians gave inordinate prominence to human wisdom, Paul devotes considerable space to contrasting true and false wisdom (1:14—4:7).

He points out that man never found God through his own wisdom. The message of reconciliation through Calvary's cross sounded ridiculous to the Greeks and scandalous to the Jews. Yet the "foolishness" of preaching the Cross brought the power of God into the lives of believing Corinthians so they overcame all sorts of wickedness. Paul's preaching was deliberately "without enticing words of man's wisdom" (2:4) as human apprehension of divine truth must come through the supernatural illumination of the Holy Spirit.

Men of Clay

Paul points up the folly of making heroes out of humans who are but servants of God. If the Corinthians would recognize them as the messengers they are, parties would not be formed to foolishly pit personalities against each other.

Paul, Apollos, and Peter were instruments in God's hand, recipients of God's gifts performing service that was ineffective apart from empowerment by God. Each one could do only a part of God's work. Though Paul "planted" and Apollos "watered" the seed of God's Word, only God gave the increase (3:6). Why exalt fallible men? Without the divine touch, some of our best service can be likened to the bungling of a child trying to help her mother.

> The baby helped shell beans today,
> Saved the waste, threw the good away.
> I've thought how patient God must be,
> When I help like she helps me.

A man visiting the countryside near Edinburgh, Scotland, took pictures of the fences bordering the farm properties. In one print his wife was seen standing beside one of the fences. A few months later he took his children to Scotland to show them the same fences, but they could not be seen. A visitor explained, "You must have been here in the spring; now it's harvest time and the grain is grown so high it blocks out the fences."

Instead of comparing their leaders, the Corinthians should have regarded them as complementary and rejoiced: "How blessed we are to have all three and the benefit of all their gifts." The spiritual harvest should have obliterated their differences. Pastors today show wisdom in inviting guest pastors, evangelists, and Bible teachers so church members may enjoy the well-rounded ministry which a variety of leaders can provide.

As servants of God, Paul, Apollos, and Peter were responsible to Him and some day answerable to Him. By frivolously approving and rejecting God's ambassadors, the Corinthians officiously usurped a prerogative of God. So Paul wrote, "Judge nothing before the time, until the Lord come . . .and then shall every man have praise of God" (4:5). Warning against judging does *not* apply to doctrinal heresy, immoral behavior, or schismatic action. The prohibition applies to secondary matters which wickedly separate brothers in Christ.

Paul put his finger on the root cause of the Corinthians factions: pride (v. 6). Self-conceit lurks in the background of such partisanship. Theologian Vernon Grounds observed: "They had done essentially the same thing which a little boy does when he identifies himself with his father. As far as that boy is concerned, he and his father are emotionally one. And, consequently, the boy resents any criticism of his father; criticism of his father is construed as criticism of the boy who has identified himself with his father" ("Christian Love and Church Problems" in *National Voice of Conservative Baptists*, Jan. 1953, p. 4).

Party-faction was so serious at Corinth that Paul devoted more space to this problem than to any other in the church. Perhaps it accentuated other problems, such as saint going to law against saint (chapter 6), the question of eating or abstaining from meat (chapters 8—10), and unkindness at the Lord's table (11:17-22).

A year later, Paul wrote at the end of his second letter to Corinth his concern that his next visit would encounter "debates, envying, wraths, strifes, backbitings, whispering, swellings, tumults'' (12:20). It led to his closing plea: ''Be of one mind, live in peace; and the God of love and peace shall be with you.'' Then he bids them to ''greet one another with an holy kiss,'' a difficult act unless they were at peace with each other (13:11-12).

At the final rehearsal for the coronation of Queen Elizabeth II, a tension-releasing incident occurred just after the orchestra had sounded the final strains. The dignified archbishop stood erect by the altar, and nearby in ranks stood officers of state. A spine-tingling fanfare of trumpets burst out signalling the queen's imminent entrance. But instead four charwomen trotted in. Pushing four carpet sweepers, they nonchalantly proceeded to circle the throne painstakingly seeking stray feathers and fuzz which had floated onto the golden carpet!

These maids had their place: their lowly service was needed to preclude a sovereign's or statesman's sneeze! But no one mistook the maids for the Queen who was to be honored.

Rather than exalt any human leader, the church must live as it sings:

> All hail the power of Jesus' name,
> Let angels prostrate fall,
> Bring forth the royal diadem
> And crown Him Lord of all.

7

Banishing In Order To Bless

The practice of shunning by a small Pennsylvania sect received newspaper prominence in 1974 through a court case. A 48-year-old potato farmer who challenged the authority of his church was punished by excommunication and by shunning, a practice in which he was avoided by all church members, including his wife of 13 years. When his civil suit against the church was heard by the Cumberland County Court, his wife and six children had been gone from their farmhouse for nine months. He testified that their 400-acre farm had fallen into disrepair, his personal life was in turmoil, and he saw his children only on weekends.

We may shudder at the extreme ostracism of this denomination's 400-year-old practice of shunning, but the New Testament does teach that believers are to withdraw fellowship from other believers for certain reasons. The more drastic form involving expulsion from membership is called excommunication; the lesser discipline is known as avoidance. This deliberate division in the church is scriptural and is necessary at times to preserve the harmony and purity of the church body. It is necessitated by spiritual conflict in an individual that threatens to infect and corrupt the whole body.

Though it is not always easy to know when a believer deserves disfellowship, certain Bible texts give basis for the practice of avoidance:

"If he refuses to listen even to the church, let him be to you as a Gentile and a tax-gatherer" (Matt. 18:17, NASB).

"Brethren, mark them which cause divisions and offenses contrary to the doctrine which ye have learned and avoid them" (Rom. 16:17).

"You must not associate with anyone who calls himself a brother but is sexually immoral or greedy.... Are you not to judge those inside?" (1 Cor. 5:11-12, NIV)

"Keep aloof from every brother who leads an unruly life and not according to the tradition which you received from us" (2 Thes. 3:6, NASB).

"A man that is an heretic after the first and second admonition reject" (Titus 3:10).

Note the words: avoid, must not associate with, keep aloof, reject. These words may be translated or paraphrased in the following ways: steer clear of, expel, disassociate, have no dealings with, shun, withdraw companionship. Interestingly, the word companion is a combination of two Latin words *with* and *bread*. A believer is not to break spiritual bread with another who has been disfellowshiped.

One mark of a healthy church is the exercise of discipline. If a church has the right to admit to membership, logically it has the power to expel. Membership which authenticates fellowship is a correlative of excommunication which ends fellowship. Disciplining which accompanies membership in a local church is paralleled by discipline which separates from membership.

Reasons for Avoidance

On what grounds should Christians withdraw fellowship from a fellow believer? Throughout church history three major reasons have been given: heresy, scandal, and schism.

Serious doctrinal error (heresy) In an adult Bible class a member who had joined the church a year previous by letter from another church denied belief in the literal, bodily resurrection of Jesus Christ. When kind and repeated attempts over a period of several weeks failed to convince him of the truth of this fundamental doctrine of the Christian faith, the church voted to erase his name from their record.

Though the peace of a church is an important matter, it is not to be peace at any price. The unity of the faith is broken by a person who denies any essential doctrine. Jude exhorts his readers to "earnestly contend for the faith which was once delivered unto the saints" (v. 3). Though not to be contentious, we are to be contenders for the truth. If a theologically liberal element begins to assert itself in a church, this group which is intruding, interfering, and interrupting by means of doctrinal aberrations should be invited to return to the once-for-all-delivered faith or leave the fellowship of the church. When a theologically liberal group becomes strong, two courses of action have been followed. One is to remain and contend for the faith; the other is to pull out and start or join a theologically sound church.

Writing to Timothy, Paul advised him to "withdraw" from those that do not hold to wholesome doctrine (1 Tim. 6:3-5). He names two men who corrupted truth by denying the doctrine of the future resurrection of the believer (2 Tim. 2:17-18).

The Apostle John showed that love has limits when he forbids giving any help to false teachers. "If there come any unto you and bring not this doctrine, receive him not into your house, neither bid him God speed (2 John 10).

Fundamental beliefs of Christianity include Christ's virgin birth, substitutionary atonement, bodily resurrection, and coming again, and the divine inspiration of Scripture. Those who deny any of these should seriously consider their right to remain within the membership of a Christian church.

Scandal A married deacon was having a romantic affair with a choir member. The pastor, getting wind of the scandal, dealt separately with each, but got no place. The board of deacons then admonished the couple, but to no avail. Ample time was given for repentance, and when none was evidenced, the deacons recommended the church drop their names from church membership. And they were removed, rightfully and scripturally so.

Good precedent for the church's action is found in the case of immorality mentioned in First Corinthians. It was reported that a man in their congregation was cohabiting with his step-mother, a sin of incest forbidden by God and untolerated even by pagans. Almost as serious was the indifference of the church in the face of this flagrant iniquity which was bringing disgrace on the cause of Christ.

So Paul directed that the man be removed from the church. The minimal meaning of his demand to "deliver such an one unto Satan" is the putting of the guilty man outside the bounds of church communion into the area dominated by the prince of this world (1 Cor. 5:5). Expulsion from Christian society would hopefully lead him to repent and subjugate his flesh by nature.

Biblical standards plainly dictate that any church member who indulges in flagrant immorality be put out of fellowship (v. 13).

At Thessalonica, some believers quit work because they thought the second coming of Christ was imminent. Their idleness led to gossiping, perhaps sponging on the church, and probably ridicule of the Gospel. Paul commands the Thessalonians to "withdraw yourselves from every brother that walketh disorderly" (2 Thes. 3:6). The man who does not work should not be fed, but rather avoided, "Note that man, and have no company with him" (vv. 11, 14).

Paul named several other sins for which fellowship should be withdrawn. Don't "keep company, if any man that is called a brother be a fornicator, or covetous, or an idolater, or a railer, or a drunkard, or an extortioner; with such an one no not to eat" (1 Cor. 5:11).

Martin Luther once threatened to excommunicate a man who

intended to sell a house for 400 gulden which he had purchased for 30. Luther suggested 150 gulden as reasonable. Though inflation had raised prices, Luther called the profit this man sought as barefaced greed deserving church discipline.

Schism After warning Titus to shun frivolous and fruitless questions that only stir up strife, Paul adds: "A man that is an heretic after the first and second admonition reject" (3:9-10). Originally, a heretic was a person who caused divisions. From the verb *to choose*, heresy at first meant a party a man chose to join, a cause he elected to promote. Heresy later became private opinion or interpretation that opposed the teaching of the Church. Paul probably uses *heretic* here in its earlier significance to refer to a factious man fomenting quarrels and disputes.

One church manual says refusal of a member to submit to church action constitutes factiousness. If he fails to heed a couple of admonitions, he will likely keep on being divisive. So, as in baseball, three strikes is out.

Another church had always taught that every believer receives the baptism of the Holy Spirit at regeneration or conversion. A dozen new people joined who believed that the baptism of the Spirit comes subsequent to salvation and is attested by the gift of tongues. This new teaching created unrest among some established members who began to feel they had not "arrived" spiritually. So the pastor and deacons met several times with the newcomers and asked them to refrain from emphasizing teaching which contradicted the official doctrine of the church. When the new group persisted in promoting their particular interpretation, almost to the point of splitting the congregation, the official board requested the resignations of the factious members.

Procedures in Avoidance

A man reportedly said, "I'm not the least bit afraid of thieves breaking into my house. I've got the place rigged so if I hear a burglar I touch a button that sends an electric current to explode the dynamite in my cellar. That will blow the burglar sky high!" We laugh at such wild schemes, but church discipline can be almost as reckless and destructive.

Admonition comes first A member guilty of heresy, scandal, or schism should usually be first approached privately by a concerned Christian. If unpersuaded from his errant ways, he should be visited by two or three who represent the church. If still unrelenting, he should be asked to answer to the whole church (Titus 3:10).

The whole church acts The exercise of discipline belongs to the whole church. Anticipating the existence of the church and an unreconcilable brother, Jesus' injunction was "tell it unto the church" (Matt. 18:17).

Paul instructs the Corinthian church to take action as a body to excommunicate the incestuous offender. "When ye are gathered together...put away from among yourselves that wicked person" (1 Cor. 5:4, 13). Paul dealt with church divisions at Corinth before he handled the matter of discipline, for a united church is essential to resolve this problem.

Avoidance is firm Avoidance establishes a relationship which convinces the disciplined brother in a firm yet loving way the seriousness of his spiritual status. No backslapping camaraderie should deceive the offender into thinking the unpleasantness will blow over by itself. A radical change is required.

A decree of disfellowship must be maintained consistently by the congregation to make the action effective. Some Christians believe social friendships with the disobedient brother must be terminated, but it seems more likely that a severance of spiritual relationships is taught. Forbidden is any conduct that would encourage the erring brother in further transgression. This is why John wrote that a false teacher should not be welcomed to a believer's home—"neither bid him God speed; for he that biddeth him God speed is partaker of his evil deeds" (2 John 10-11). Opposition to grievous sin must be plainly expressed.

But love does not stop To refuse hospitality to a false teacher is not to endorse unkindness or discourtesy. If a heretical teacher were hungry and shelterless, certainly John does not forbid him the ordinary courtesies of life. Only in his official capacity is a false teacher not to receive help.

A *Christianity Today* (August 31, 1962) article described a small group in Britain that practiced extreme separation from "nonbelievers" (those voted out of the fellowship). A 73-year-old man reportedly had been compelled to leave his wife after 37 years of happy married life. The distraught woman was labeled a "sinner" and the home "leprous." A press report told of a 21-year-old who committed suicide after his parents were ordered by this group to have no social contact with him. Because believers and "unbelievers" are not supposed to eat together, one account tells how righteousness was fulfilled by sawing a table in half so that it was technically two tables, though the halves were never parted.

But redemptive avoidance cannot mean such cutting off of all contact with offenders. After Paul commanded Christians not to keep company with disorderly idlers, he added: "Yet count him not as an enemy, but admonish him as a brother" (2 Thes. 3:15). How can one admonish a brother if he shuns him completely? In the hope of helping a brother be restored to God's way, normal civility, evident concern, and regular dialogue are to be maintained. Corporate activities of a spiritual nature are to be denied the unrepentant offender.

Neither does avoidance mean renunciation of family ties. Some Christians at Corinth concluded that the spiritual chasm between a believer and an unbelieving mate called for the breakup of the marriage, but Paul affirmed the opposite. Rather, the continuance of the relationship provides opportunity of witness to the unbeliever. Prudent avoidance discreetly uses natural, social, and marital associations to remind the offender of his need and point him back to spiritual fellowship.

Avoidance must walk a straight line that simultaneously affirms two truths: first, that a wayward believer has forfeited the privileges of fellowship by persisting in false and unrighteous ways; second, that he has an open invitation to return to fellowship upon repentance. Avoidance has been called "both excommunication and communication." When one is lacking, avoidance fails.

Purpose of Avoidance

At least three purposes are served by withdrawal of fellowship, the last being the most important.

To refine the church When Paul rebuked the Corinthians for failure to deal with the case of immorality in their midst, he asked, "Don't you know how a little yeast can permeate the whole lump?" then urged them to "clear out every bit of the old yeast that you may be a new unleavened bread!" (1 Cor. 5:6-7, PH)

Just as one sickly lamb may spread disease through an entire flock, or one little spark kindle a major fire, so one case of evil unchecked may spread spiritual disease all through a congregation. To stop the contagion before it infected the whole Corinthian body, the offender was to be expelled.

To dispel any impression of church corruption When any church member is allowed to persist in heresy, scandal, or schism, the outside world is given a wrong concept of the church. Continuation of wrongdoing leads outsiders to think the church is unconcerned with righteousness, and the scandal spreads: "The church is full of hypocrites."

Since the reputation of the church depends on the lives of its members, discipline is required when any member goes astray in order to show the community that God honors truth and purity.

To restore the erring brother Undoubtedly the major purpose of avoidance is remedial, the repentance and restoration of the miscreant. Expulsion seems harsh, but is meant as a ministry. For if the sinning brother, whose life is warped and unhappy, can be led back to the fold through withdrawal of fellowship, then chords that were broken will vibrate once more in harmony and happiness. Like earthly fathers, the heavenly Father doesn't punish His children to torture them, but to correct them.

To show the purpose of avoidance, Paul uses expressions such as "that they may learn not to blaspheme" (1 Tim. 1:20), "that he may be ashamed" (2 Thes. 3:14), and "that the spirit may be saved" (1 Cor. 5:5). The last measure refers to the incestuous Corinthian whom Paul told the church to put out of membership. Restoration is the goal Paul wished to see achieved through excommunication.

That the brother did repent seems clear from Paul's second letter to the Corinthians. Perhaps on the arrival of his first letter, the church took action which had its desired effect. In fact, they may have been too harsh in their treatment and too slow to welcome back the offender, for Paul writes: "Sufficient to such a man is this punishment, which was inflicted of many. So that contrariwise ye ought rather to forgive him, and comfort him, lest perhaps such a one should be swallowed up with overmuch sorrow" (2 Cor. 2:6-7).

A judicious balance must be followed between avoidance and involvement, between separating and socializing. This can be achieved as we steadfastly love both God and man, and fervently hate evil.

8

Bigger Than Big Personalities

What would you think of a church that struggled through three "fights" or flare-ups in a short span of years? This happened to the vibrant New Testament church at Antioch in Syria. Did these clashes cripple the testimony of that church to the community and world?

The church at Antioch was where the peerless Barnabas and Paul taught for a year, where irrepressible believers were first called Christians, where relief funds were collected for the famine-stricken saints in Jerusalem and Judea, and where the first missionaries to the Gentile world were commissioned. Despite these spiritual accomplishments, Antioch was the scene of three serious disagreements.

Two of the quarrels have already been discussed: the acute dissension over the question of faith-plus-works that led to the first Jerusalem council; and the sharp controversy over Mark that ruptured the partnership between Paul and Barnabas. Now we encounter the head-to-head showdown between the two leading apostles, Peter and Paul.

Does the occurrence of sharp squabbles in the Antiochan church demonstrate a lack of spirituality? Not necessarily. It probably demonstrates that here was a church—and leadership—

willing to admit their differences and seek reconciliation rather than pretending these differences didn't exist and hoping they would fade away. The further a church advances, the greater the likelihood of disagreements and conflicts. The presence of problems may indicate carnality, but at Antioch problems were a sign of progress against evil.

Leader against Leader

This altercation squared off the two leading personalities in the New Testament. C. Peter Wagner calls the incident "one of the Scripture's best-known heavyweight fights." The title is deserved on two counts: not only are top-flight "contenders" involved, but the "heaviness" of the issue concerns the heart of the Gospel.

On one side we have Peter, generally recognized as number one among Jesus' twelve disciples, not without reason. He is named first on every list of disciples; he was their spokesman; he chaired the election of a successor to Judas; he was the eloquent preacher on the Day of Pentecost; and he was the first to proclaim the Gospel to Gentiles in the house of Cornelius. He is involved in almost every significant action in the first twelve chapters of Acts except the stories of deacons Stephen and Philip.

On the other side is the redoubtable Paul. As Peter fades from the pages of Acts, Paul enters as the dominant character. His journeys and journals comprise a major part of the New Testament. He wrote about half the New Testament books. In fact, outside the four Gospels, the first half of Acts, the Book of Revelation, and a few short letters, Paul's deeds and words make up the New Testament.

To debate who is the greater apostle might lead to the error of the Corinthian party spirit which queues up believers in support of one human leader like fans cheering for a favorite quarterback.

Though we read much more about Paul than Peter in the New Testament, we should not conclude that Peter's ministry diminishes after the first church council. From mid-Acts on, the Holy Spirit's purpose is to trace the outreach of the Church across the Roman empire through Paul and his helpers. Certainly Peter's place as foremost disciple during Jesus' earthly ministry, plus his forceful leadership during the early years of apostolic history, have established him near the pinnacle of biblical greatness. We must be careful not to overreact against certain church traditions which unscripturally elevate him to primacy.

We do not learn of Paul's rebuke of Peter in the historical record of Acts, but from Paul's report in his letter to the Galatians. He states: "But when Cephas (Peter) came to Antioch, I opposed him to his face, because he stood condemned" (2:11). The reason Paul included this incident was that false teachers were questioning his authority as an apostle. They tried to undermine his teaching by asserting his inferiority to the other disciples who had been trained by Jesus.

So Paul defends his special apostleship in the first two chapters of Galatians by three declarations:

Paul did not get his message from the other apostles, but by direct revelation from Jesus Christ (1:11-24).

When Paul did consult with the "pillars" of the church at Jerusalem, including Apostles Peter and John, at least a dozen years after his dramatic conversion, Paul's beliefs were promptly acknowledged as the true Gospel (2:1-10).

When the Apostle Peter compromised the purity of the Gospel by his conduct, Paul rebuked him openly. This marked the highest level of apostolic authority, and Peter's acceptance of correction destroys any doctrine of apostolic infallibility or popish supremacy of Peter.

A Leader Rebuked

At Antioch Peter had been eating with Gentile believers and disregarding the cultural dietary laws of the Jews. His conduct made it plain that Gentiles need not observe the Jewish traditions in order to be accepted by God. But when Jewish believers arrived from Jerusalem, Peter avoided eating with the Gentiles in deference to the tradition-bound Jewish Christians. He acted hypocritically.

Peter's actions spoke louder than words. He was saying by his behavior what the Judaizers taught by precept: the Jewish food laws should be observed by "good Christians"; or else he was silently saying that he feared loss of status among the Jewish believers.

How hard it is to change! Old habits cling tightly, even to apostles. Despite a special vision which prepared Peter to witness to the Gentile family of Cornelius: "God hath showed me that I should not call any man common or unclean" (Acts 10:28), he yielded to human prejudice rather than God's direction. Paul quickly saw the inconsistency.

As usual, the leader's action carried others with it, even Barnabas who had been the encourager of the Gentile believers at Antioch from the beginning. The implications were staggering. Not only was a stigma of ceremonial uncleanness cast over Gentile Christians, but observers might conclude that the laws of Moses were indispensable for acceptance by God. Peter's action was an unintentional denial of the Gospel of grace. This fissure in basic doctrine could not be bridged by silence in hopes of maintaining a spurious unity.

Scholars disagree as to whether this event took place before or after the Jerusalem council, but it seems likely to have occurred previously, for Paul would otherwise have referred to the council's verdict in reproving Peter. Peter's equivocating seems almost impossible after the council at which he firmly upheld salvation for Gentiles apart from what he called "the yoke of the law" (Acts 15:7-11).

Paul issued a strong rebuke, charging Peter with glaring inconsistency. Said Paul, "I withstood him to the face." *Withstood* means "to set one's self against." This is the same verb used when we are told to *resist* the devil. And, Paul flatly called him guilty because "he was to be blamed" (Gal. 2:11).

The extent of the rebuke is difficult to discern, but Paul's commentary here (2:14-18), gives the nature and explanation of the reproof. A reconstruction of the points shows the serious implications of Peter's action. Paul was saying, in effect, "Peter, you are returning to the Law, an intolerable burden which can never justify anyone."

Veteran Bible teacher Ralph L. Keiper paraphrases these verses graphically: "Peter, I smell ham on your breath. You forgot your Certs. There was a time when you wouldn't eat ham as part of your hope of salvation. Then after you trusted Christ, it didn't matter if you ate ham. But now when the no-ham eaters have come from Jerusalem you have gone back to your kosher ways. But the smell of ham still lingers on your breath. You are most inconsistent. You are compelling Gentile believers to observe Jewish law which can never justify anyone."

"Peter, by returning to the law, you undercut strength for godly living" (2:19-20).

The law gives no power to overcome sin. But by identifying with Christ a person enters upon a new life. "I am crucified with Christ . . .but Christ lives in me," says Paul. To return to the Law is to forsake the source of power.

"Peter, you make the death of Christ superfluous" (2:21).

The final clause of the rebuke (or its commentary) makes a drastic claim. If righteousness—the way to heaven and standing with God—comes by keeping the law, why did Christ come to earth to die? "Peter, you are going back to a system that rules out the cross of Christ; and we could charge God with utmost cruelty in sending His Son to die if His death were unnecessary."

A Leader's Goal

In this same Galatian letter Paul wrote, "Brethren, if a man be overtaken in a fault, ye which are spiritual, restore such an one in the spirit of meekness; considering thyself, lest thou also be tempted'' (6:1). Paul did not hesitate to reprove his brother of a grievous fault, but he focused on the all-important issue and he genuinely cared about Peter.

Believers are commanded to admonish, exhort, reprimand, and correct one another—or figuratively, to wash one another's feet. Washing the saints' feet in a spiritual sense has come to mean helping our fellow Christians get rid of moral defilement accumulated in daily walk, as well as humbly serving them.

As Paul ''washed Peter's feet'' in this particular circumstance, he followed procedures that are important for us in the same kind of service.

Make sure your brother's feet are dirty. A young businesswoman arrived half an hour late to speak to a Bible study group. Immediately the friend who invited her took her aside and admonished her for keeping these first-time-attending, non-Christian neighbors waiting for so long. Then the businesswoman explained, ''My car was hit by a drunken driver. I could not leave till the police came, also a wrecker for my badly damaged car. I should have gone to the hospital, for I ache all over, but I refused the ambulance driver and got a taxi here.''

We should never get the wash basin ready until we have the facts straight. We should make sure our brother has definitely committed a trespass before attempting to correct him. Paul had full information on Peter's withdrawal from Gentile fellowship, and knew his feet needed washing.

See that your own hands are clean. In some sections of Scotland, bachelor friends of the bridegroom grab him the night before a wedding and carry him to a convenient spot for removing his shoes and socks and pretending to wash his feet. But everyone who dips his hand in the water has first blackened it with soot. Result—the groom's feet become dirtier than ever.

Whatever the significance of that custom, the person who tries to wash a fellow believer's feet with stains on his own hands will botch the job. Paraphrasing some advice of Jesus, "First wash your own hands, then you shall see clearly to wash your brother's feet."

In a Connecticut city 53 residents of a certain area signed a petition to stop reckless driving on their streets. The police set a watch and a few nights later five violators were caught. All five were signers of the complaint!

Paul's hands were clean in the matter of justification through faith without works of the law. When pressure was exerted on him to circumcize Titus as a convert to the Christian-Hebrew church, Paul resisted in order to uphold the essential truth of the Gospel (Gal. 2:3-5). It is those "which are spiritual" who are to restore brethren that stumble.

Do foot-washing in the proper place. The footwasher should never sound a trumpet before announcing, "I'm about to set Brother X straight." Foot-washing is not an exhibition of dirt or failure. When renewal meetings at a Christian college led to open confession of sins that seemed to wallow in shame, the president wisely closed the service. We are to wash feet, not splatter the filth about.

On some occasions foot-washing should be public: private wrongs require private righting, and public wrongs demand public correction. For those who sin openly, the command is, "Rebuke before all" (1 Tim. 5:20). Since Peter's duplicity was public and widely influential, Paul's correction must be "before them all" (Gal. 2:14).

Stoop low. To wash feet, you have to kneel as Jesus did to wash the disciples' feet. You cannot strut like a drill officer nor parade like a peacock when you're washing feet. Restoration should be done "considering thyself, lest thou also be tempted." We may assume that Paul's reproof was without a superior attitude, but with genuine humility before the Lord.

John Wesley and a preacher-friend of plain habits were invited to dinner where the host's daughter, noted for her beauty, had been profoundly impressed by Wesley's preaching. During a pause in the meal, Wesley's friend took the young lady's hand and called attention to the sparkling rings she wore. "What do you think of this, sir, for a Methodist hand?" The girl turned crimson. Wesley likewise was embarrassed, for his aversion to jewelry was well-known. But with a benevolent smile, he simply said, "The hand is very beautiful." Wesley's remark both cooled the too-hot water poured by his friend, and made the foot-washing gentle. The young lady appeared at the evening service without her jewels, and became a strong Christian.

Someone said, "When you start heaving rocks of truth at people, be sure to wrap them in packages of love." Paul must have spoken the truth to Peter in love, though vigorously.

Dry them. After the Lord washed the disciples' feet, He wiped them. Without a thorough job of drying, damp feet contacting dirt can make the feet muddier than before the washing. Restoring an erring brother involves drying his feet so he may again walk the paths of righteousness—we must forgive and forget.

In a Canadian church an elder resigned from the board because of a brief lapse to his pre-conversion alcoholism. After years of sobriety, he was seen intoxicated on a public vehicle. His resignation was noted in the official minutes of the elder board. Some months later at a mid-week meeting, he confessed the failure and asked forgiveness of the church. He was soon voted back to the elder board. Not long after, the elders voted to expunge from their record every mention of the incident, so that today not a word of his fault appears in the official minutes. That body of believers thoroughly dried the offender's feet.

F. B. Meyer in his book, *Love to the Uttermost*, says, "We do not often enough wash one another's feet. We are conscious of the imperfections of those around us; we are content to note and criticize them. We dare not attempt to remove them, partly because we do not love with a love like Christ's, and partly because we are not willing to stoop low enough. None is able to restore those that are overtaken in a fault who does not count himself the chief of sinners and the least of saints. We need more of this lowly, loving spirit."

Still a Leader

An ordinary leader could have reacted vehemently against Paul's criticism. Protecting his reputation could have triggered an angry defense, no matter what the merits of the issue. And the church could have been splintered by a fierce collision of its leaders.

But Peter reacted, it seems, the same way he had responded to previous reproofs. Peter characteristically acknowledged his errors immediately and without reservation. The night he thrice denied the Lord, the gaze of Jesus' eyes when the cock crowed was more than Peter could bear. He went out into the night weeping tears of remorse. Impetuous in his words and ways, he was just as hasty to mend his wrongs. Not a word indicates that he acted otherwise here.

Peter's acceptance of Paul's reprimand is an example to all for receiving a rebuke with Christian grace. No sharp retort. No self-seeking defense. God's truth is knowable, and it is absolute. In his heart Peter knew he had been wrong, and he perceived the damage of his action. It is likely he rejoined Gentile believers at mealtime that very day. At the Jerusalem council Peter strongly supported Paul's position on salvation apart from Moses' law, and years later he wrote a letter referring to "our beloved brother Paul" (2 Peter 3:15).

Who was the winner of this "heavyweight bout"? It was no contest, because Peter put up no fight. But the fight that was avoided permitted the ongoing flow of the pure Gospel and the entire Church body was winner!

9

We Are Our Brother's Keeper

Someone wrote,

For me to love the world—no chore;
My problem—the neighbor next door.

During a midweek Sunday School teachers' meeting, Archie, a teacher in the adult department, snapped at Jonathan, the superintendent. His remarks were not only sharp but unnecessarily personal. Archie thought he saw hurt in Jonathan's face, but didn't see how he could take it seriously. He felt an impulse to apologize, but brushed it aside. On Saturday evening Archie was preparing his class lesson when he recalled those unkind words spouted at Jonathan. Should he do anything now about the incident?

Though the Church is one spiritual family, joined together as the body of Christ, sometimes brothers become unbrotherly, resulting in strained situations or broken relationships. Our Lord spoke several times about brother being at odds with brother. What comes through loud and clear is that it is sin for brothers to continue in an alienated state. Jesus instructs both the offending, guilty party, and the offended, innocent party to seek reconciliation. God holds both parties responsible for the rift.

The Duty of the Offender

In the Sermon on the Mount Jesus said, "If you are offering your gift at the altar and there remember that your brother has something against you, leave your gift there in front of the altar. First go and be reconciled to your brother, and then come and offer your gift" (Matt. 5:23-24, NIV).

Here's the biblical picture. A worshiper brings a lamb to the outer court of the temple to wait his turn till the officiating priest can receive the animal and sacrifice it in the inner court. In these moments only the most pressing matter would justify the withdrawal of the worshiper before offering the lamb. But in the holy hush he suddenly recalls that recently he unjustly denounced a brother. Jesus teaches that he should forego worship and be reunited with his brother.

Jesus is not urging a habitual introspection at our worship services, nor is He suggesting that we postpone reconciliation till our regular Communion services. The point is that if we have delayed making peace, we would do well to postpone even the most solemn worship to go on a peace mission. Apparently worship will not be wholehearted if we are at odds with a brother. To reconcile is better than sacrifice, is Jesus' paraphrase of the Old Testament admonition to obey.

But it is not a matter of reconciliation instead of worship, rather reconciliation in order to worship. Our love and adoration to God will be purer because of restored love with our fellow man.

A lad was praying at grandmother's knee: "If I should die before I wake, I pray . . ." His voice trailed off.

"Go on, Johnny," Grandmother's voice prompted.

The little boy jumped to his feet. "Wait a minute," he exclaimed, then hurried down the stairs. In a few moments he was back to finish the prayer. When Grandma questioned the little form tucked in bed, he exclaimed, "I began to think what I was praying. I set up brother's wooden soldiers on their heads to see him get mad in the morning. But if I should die before I wake, I didn't want him to find the mess, so had to go and fix them.''

Grandma's comment was, ''You did right. I imagine a good many prayers would be helped by stopping in the middle to undo a wrong.''

The Church of England Communion service includes this caution: ''Ye that. . .are in love and charity with your neighbors. . .draw near with faith.''

Returning to the problem of Archie, the teacher who suddenly remembered his insulting words to Jonathan, there was something to be done. He got in his car and drove over to Jonathan's home, blurted out a sincere apology, and asked forgiveness. Jonathan admitted his simmering bitterness, and together they prayed. Both found their Sunday School duties a delight the next morning.

The Duty of the Offended

Was there anything that Jonathan should have done, though he was the innocent, yelled-at, offended party? The New Testament has some definite rules for dealing with a brother who has wronged us.

First, be slow to take offense. A well-known Canadian preacher, asked the secret for happy marriages, replied, ''Five bears—bear and forbear.'' The shrewd Ben Franklin advised: ''Write injuries in dust, benefits in marble.'' Paul wrote that we should be ''forbearing one another in love'' (Eph. 4:2). We can overlook many slights and even indignities by the grace of Christ.

If we suffer what we consider unkindness or injustice from a fellow believer, perhaps a recognition of their personal or business stresses will help us to sympathize and readily forgive.

Forbearance with our brothers rules out scorekeeping of wrongs suffered. It does not make trophies out of hurt feelings, polishing and displaying them by reliving the hurts. Forbearance with love makes it possible to shrug off nasty things and not count them offenses.

In *The Hiding Place*, author Corrie ten Boom describes a reunion after a separation from her sister, Betsie, in a Nazi concentration camp. Corrie could see that her sister's face was swollen. Corrie asked if a guard had beaten her, and she was amazed at Betsie's answer: "I felt so sorry for that man." What loving forbearance!

A widely used church covenant has members promising each other "to be slow to take offense, but always ready for reconciliation, and mindful of the rules of our Saviour, to secure it without delay." What are the Saviour's rules?

Go to the person who has wronged you. If the offense is serious enough to need righting, you should go directly and privately to the offender and ask him to correct the wrong. This is Jesus' counsel: "If thy brother shall trespass against thee, go and tell him his fault between thee and him!" (Matt. 18:15)

On a stone block built into a wall of Quebec City post office is carved the picture of a dog gnawing a bone. Originally placed over the door of a murdered man, the picture and accompanying words threaten revenge on nameless assailants:

I am a dog that gnaws his bone,
I crouch and gnaw it all alone;
The time will come, which is not yet,
When I'll bite him by whom I'm bit.

How harmful it is to mull over wrongs done us, "gnawing bones" of bitterness, poisoning our souls. And the unrighted wrong continues to handicap the offended's life until it is properly removed. It is your duty to get it off your chest.

How easy for brothers at odds to reason that the other should make the first move. The offender reasons, "He deserves what he got. If it was so bad, he'll let me know and then I'll make things right." The offended one thinks, "He is so crude, it wouldn't do any good to talk to him—I'd rather stay away from his kind." Both are wrong, according to Jesus. And both are hurting the body of Christ.

A girl said, "Ten years ago my mother and uncle had a bitter fight and they stopped seeing each other. My mother missed him greatly. And I'm sure my uncle missed her too, for they had been like two peas in a pod. Recently when my mother became ill, my uncle heard of it and came to visit with a bouquet of flowers. Now they are the best of friends again." How sad for relatives to miss years of good times through alienation. The Bible speaks of prompt reconciliation: "Let not the sun go down upon your wrath" (Eph. 4:26).

Counselors tell us of two wrong, harmful ways to handle anger, and a third, healing way. To bottle up anger internally is to strain both our emotional and physical systems. But to vent anger unrestrainedly is to destroy a relationship. So what do we do?

Realistically admit: "I am getting angry; I don't want to be angry, so please help me with this anger."

To convince a person that he has done wrong may be a difficult and delicate assignment. Argument may develop. Self-control, humility, and love are the most convincing "arguments" the offended can have. In reality, the health of the Christian body is at stake.

The offense may have some logical explanation, or not be as bad as it seemed before discussion. The confrontation may bring new significant facts to light. But if the injury is real and hurtful, and your brother agrees he was wrong, and asks forgiveness, then "thou has gained thy brother" (Matt. 18:15). Not the case, but your *brother*! And the conflict need not be known beyond the two concerned.

A well-known Bible teacher holding meetings in California made a sneering remark about a denomination which he believed taught wrong doctrine in secondary matters. Afterward a preacher in that denomination sought an interview with the Bible teacher and stated his grievance. The teacher quickly apologized, and to make amends he asked the minister to invite several fellow ministers of that denomination to a guest luncheon. At the table the offender began, "We know we have certain doctrinal differences, but during lunch today let's discuss only those points on which we agree. First, do we agree that Jesus Christ is God?" There was unanimous assent. They began to talk about what the Lord Jesus meant to them. As the meal progressed, tension relaxed and a deepening fellowship followed. Parting, they promised to pray for one another.

Confrontation and repentance made it true:
I was angry with my friend,
I told my wrath, my wrath did end.

Enlist the help of other brothers. If a private, personal approach proves fruitless, the next step is clear. Jesus said, "But if he does not listen to you, take one or two more with you, so that by the mouth of two or three witnesses every fact may be confirmed" (Matt. 18:16, NASB).

The added number may reinforce the influence to convict the wrongdoer of his offense. Added counselors provide added wisdom. Most congregations have some sensitive and seasoned saints who, neither protagonist nor antagonist, can act objectively as referees. These arbitrators need not hold formal office in the church, but because of tactful manner and the wisdom of experience may be instruments of peace.

Paul spoke sharply to believers who took their differences before a secular court. Instead of dishonoring their Lord by this means, they should be willing to suffer wrong (1 Cor. 6:7), or to seek out Christian arbiters to listen to both sides and render a settlement. Paul chided the Corinthians, "Is it so, that there is not a wise man among you? No, not one that shall be able to judge between his brethren?" (v. 5)

If this conference of informal judges cannot settle the matter because the erring party will not listen and apologize or make restitution, the counselors will be witnesses before the church. The offense has reached a very serious stage at this point.

Bring it before the church. One church covenant reads: "We will not bring to the church a complaint against any member for personal trespass or offence until we have taken the first and second steps pointed out by Christ, thus endeavoring to settle all private offences without publicity."

When the matter comes before the church, both brothers should be present and permitted to present their cases. If the offender is judged wrong by the congregation and he still refuses to make the wrong right, he is to be disfellowshiped. The offence is harmful, but to stubbornly refuse conciliation is to subvert the very life of the fellowship. Jesus' verdict is severe: "If he refuses to listen to the church, let him be to you as a Gentile and a tax-gatherer" (Matt. 18:17, NASB).

Forgive the repentant brother. Soon after dealing with the erring brother, Jesus speaks of forgiveness. He advocates readiness to forgive great and oft-repeated offences. The instruction arises from Peter's question, "Lord how oft shall my brother sin against me, and I forgive him?" (v. 21) Peter suggested a number which he thought magnanimous: "seven times." Jesus' answer of "seventy times seven" does not recommend scorekeeping till a limit of 490, but of unending forgiveness to those who ask it. God sets no limit on the times He forgives us!

Jesus makes a strong case for honest, prompt confrontation between brothers at odds. He makes an equally strong case for full, loving, repeated forgiveness. This nurtures and restores the love among Christians which Jesus said is evidence to the world that He is our Saviour and God is our Father (John 13:35).

When Moravian missionaries first went to the Eskimos, they could not find a word in the Eskimos' language for "forgiveness." So they made one up. The long compound meant literally, "not-being-able-to-think-about-it-anymore." True forgiveness may not always completely remove a wound from the memory, but it does transform the recollected grudge to thanksgiving.

Paul's counsel to the Colossian church helps make Christian brotherhood a reality: "As those who have been chosen of God, holy and beloved, put on a heart of compassion, kindness, humility, gentleness and patience; bearing with one another, and forgiving each other, whoever has a complaint against any one; just as the Lord forgave you, so also should you. And beyond all these things put on love, which is the perfect bond of unity. And let the peace of God rule in your hearts, to which indeed you were called in one body; and be thankful" (3:12-15, NASB).

10
Ladies, Have a Heart!

A story is told of two unmarried sisters who had so bitter a ruckus they stopped speaking to each other. Unable or unwilling to leave their small home, they continued to use the same rooms and sleep in the same bedroom. A chalk line divided the sleeping area into two halves, separating doorway and fireplace, so that each could come and go and get her own meals without trespassing on her sister's domain. In the black of night each could hear the breathing of the foe. For years they co-existed in grinding silence. Neither was willing to take the first step to reconciliation.

Two women at the church in Philippi had a rift, probably of a mild nature, but to prevent it from becoming a major rupture Paul spoke to the women in his letter to that church.

Women played an important role in the early Church. Some of them gave financial support to Jesus' ministry (Luke 8:1-3). Grieving women were last to leave Jesus' cross and first to discover the empty tomb. In the last chapter of Romans, Paul lists nearly 30 names of co-workers, one-third of which are women's. On some mission fields today women workers outnumber men; the "fairer, weaker sex" has proved its selflessness and strength, many in worse situations than men.

The female element loomed large in the Philippian church.

Paul's first congregation was composed of women meeting by the riverside. His first convert was Lydia, a lady merchant (Acts 16:13-14). Then a demon-possessed girl was healed and saved (v. 18). Among early members were the two women who had a falling out, Euodias and Syntyche. They may have been from the nobility, as were many of Paul's female converts (17:4, 12). They had been diligent co-workers of Paul's from near the beginning, making a significant contribution in those formative years of this outstanding church.

We should not be surprised that this flourishing congregation had a spat or more between its folk. Disagreements are inevitable in the best of churches. The real problem is the proper resolution of unavoidable disputes.

Minor Tiff or Major Trauma?

Somehow Satan got his claws hooked in, not so much that discord separated two warmhearted women, but that it went unmended too long. In a thriving church like Philippi, slight bickerings would rumble like thunder. Paul's appeal indicates that the difference was not simply a private matter but one that threatened the unity of the congregation.

Incidentally, this is the sole New Testament case of dissension with women as the principals. Even the first friction that involved widows brought confrontation between male Hebrews and male Hellenists.

On what did these women differ? We are not told. Conflicts can be classified under two main categories: substantive, and interpersonal. Conflict occurs when two ideas or actions try to occupy the same operating space at the same time. For example, if a member asserts that the best way to evangelize is by house-to-house visitation, and another insists that joining protest marches is the proper method, conflict will result. This is substantive conflict.

Interpersonal conflict stems from incompatibility between

people rather than from facts and values. Examples would be dislike because of differences, real and imagined wrongs done, or envious and competitive reactions. Interpersonal antagonism cannot be easily differentiated from substantive conflict because each subtly interacts with the other.

The discord between the Philippian ladies may have related to doctrine, ethics, or worship, perhaps over some small point. Whether or not it had a substantive basis, it flared into interpersonal conflict.

How easy for division to start over some jot or tittle, like the better word to use in liturgy. Two churches of differing denominations in a community tried to join forces to form one church. But they could not agree on whether to say, "Forgive us our debts" or "Forgive us our trespasses." So the newspaper reported that one church went back to their trespasses while the other returned to their debts!

How easy to become convinced that our method is the only right way. Two ministers, each convinced of his own denominational program's superiority, engaged in good-natured banter. "Who's really to say which is the better," commented one of the ministers. "After all, we both do the Lord's work." "Yes," replied the other with a twinkle, "you do it in your way, and I in His."

Two godly, energetic people who do not walk close to God can push each other into Satan's service. These devout women had a disagreement, neglected to settle it lovingly, began to avoid each other, and perhaps criticized each other to friends. Doubtless both were pained by the alienation, but neither initiated a reconciliation.

Paul wished these two women to compose their differences before the issue grew to serious proportions, disrupting the fellowship, strengthening the enemy, and becoming the laughingstock of the city. The following lines express what should have happened:

"Yes, you did too!"
"I did not!"
Thus the little quarrel started,
Thus, by unkind little words,
Two fond friends were parted.
"I am sorry."
"So am I."
Thus the little quarrel ended,
Thus, by loving little words,
Two fond hearts were mended.

An Urgent Plea

Paul pleads with each lady separately, first Euodias, then Syntyche. The verb is repeated, "I *beseech* Euodias, and I *beseech* Syntyche." He handles the names alphabetically—perhaps unintentionally—like the listing of credits to a TV program, or of speakers at a Bible conference. Paul shows no partiality.

These names have been found over 20 times in ancient inscriptions. Euodias means "prosperous journey" or "fragrance." Syntyche means "pleasant acquaintance," or "happy chance." Someone labeled them Mrs. Fragrance and Mrs. Fortunate; another facetiously called them Mrs. Odious and Mrs. Soon-touchy.

At any rate, Paul's appeal is strong. The root of "beseech" gives us the Comforter, a title for the Third Member of the Trinity (John 16:7). Paul's entreaty here echoes the Holy Spirit, coming alongside to help.

Paul exhorts these two ladies to "be of the same mind in the Lord" (Phil 4:2). He had prepared them for this appeal by a similar, general command in the earlier part of the letter: "Be like-minded, having the same love, being of one accord, of one mind" (2:2). In fact, the entire second chapter of Philippians is devoted to the kind of mind every believer should have—the mind of Christ, which was one of humility. Because things equal to the same thing are equal to each other, if Euodias and Syntyche can both have the mind of Christ, they will indeed be like-minded, and lowly-minded, which will lead to reconciliation.

The section that illustrates the mind of Christ (2:5-8) is the classic passage on His self-humbling. No other paragraph in the Bible compasses in so short a span and with such phraseology so much truth on the condescension of the Son of God. Paul's purpose in these verses is not to provide subtle theological dogma, but to illustrate Christian duty. We ought to have the kind of mind displayed in the utter self-emptying of Christ: from the throne of God to the grave of a criminal, including from God to man (while still retaining deity), from Master to servant, from life to death (the shameful death reserved for aliens, slaves, and criminals).

As Christ stooped, so should we stoop, getting rid of pride, which is the cause of so many disputes. If Euodias and Syntyche would allow Christ's lowly-mindedness to flood their minds, their conflict would end. In connection with this self-emptying passage Paul wrote, "Let nothing be done through strife or vainglory; but in lowliness of mind let each esteem other better than themselves. Look not every man on his own things, but every man also on the things of others" (2:3-4). Perhaps he had Euodias and Syntyche in mind when he so wrote.

After writing of the humility of Christ, Paul said, "Do all things without murmurings and disputings" (2:14). The ladies needed to take heed. In the light of Christ's self-effacement, how small and petty were their differences! How quickly they should have put away trifling animosities and ill-will, and in the spirit of humility sought peace.

Paul's appeal "in the Lord" means as members of His body, in the consciousness of His presence, moved by His love, submitting to His guidance, strongly desiring to please Him, possessing His spirit of lowliness.

When Paul's letter arrived at Philippi, the church assembled, eager to hear from their beloved founder. Those present may have included Lydia and her household, the formerly demon-possessed girl, the jailer and his family, many other converts, and Euodias and Syntyche. All would be listening attentively as they heard Paul's words of confidence and encouragement. When the leader read, "Do all things without murmurings and disputings," both Euodias and Syntyche looked straight ahead. Then, suddenly, a little later and without warning, "I beseech Euodias"—and she almost jumped out of her seat. " . . .and I beseech Syntyche"—and there was a squeal from her side. And they both strained to hear what came next: "that they be of the same mind in the Lord." In other words, "Patch up your quarrel!" What a jolt!

This public admonition in the letter probably produced embarrassment, but it was nothing like the humiliation to be suffered in the day of judgment when God will open His books to reveal the record of human deeds for which we must answer. Though the guilt of our sins has been cancelled through the cross of Christ, we still have to stand before the judgment seat of Christ to account for works since our regeneration, either to receive reward or suffer loss (2 Cor. 5:10). Perhaps we'll be shamed to hear our name called out in connection with a wrong done another believer which we have never righted. But that is avoidable, for "if we would judge ourselves, we should not be judged" (1 Cor. 11:31).

More Help Needed

Recently, a Jewish engineer, meditating at Jerusalem's Western (Wailing) Wall, became alarmed at growing clumps of weeds hanging from the crannies of the huge stones. His training told him that the weeds could eventually tumble the wall. His warning aroused a controversy in Israel, especially when the nation's two chief rabbis, possessing equal ecclesiastical authority, took opposite views. One said, because the weeds symbolize the ruin of the

Temple, they must not be plucked. The other, sensing the potential damage to the wall, urged they be plucked but left near the Wall as reminder of the Temple's destruction. When the two rabbis reached an impasse, Israel's Custodian of Holy Places was asked what he would do. His cagey answer: "Get a third opinion."

As we saw earlier, believers at odds who are unable to reconcile in private session are to call on arbiter-witnesses. Here Paul asked a "true yokefellow" to act as third party, perhaps in full expectation that he can help calm this tempest in a teapot.

Who was this fellow worker? Some think the word yokefellow here is a proper name—Synsugus, just as the ladies' names are definite. Others guess him to be the husband of either Euodias or Syntyche, or that Paul refers to Epaphroditus, Timothy, Silas, or even Luke, whose home was supposed to be Philippi. Whoever—it had to be a person of discretion and honor to bring together these women at variance. To heal dissension and promote Christian unity is a delicate, noble work and a needed ministry.

If a dispute involves members of the same church, the referee should probably be a member of that fellowship too. If a problem concerns two believers from different churches, the third party should be someone with a relationship to both parties, perhaps one of the pastors, or an elder.

A pastor in an eastern city, realizing feuding had gone on among the preachers and Christian organizations in his city, decided on a daring plan. He phoned a dozen leaders, inviting them to lunch with him in a downtown club, not telling any that the others were coming. As each man entered the private dining room, he saw another or others to whom he had not spoken for months or years. In some cases the feuds had been intense. After the blessing, the host pastor frankly told his reason for getting them together and asked if something could be done about the ugly divisions. Before long, most were on their knees in prayer.

Two who had been most bitterly at odds shook hands. Only one man said he could not ask the Lord to bless the endeavor, feeling that some present were guilty of compromise. But the rest rediscovered their oneness in Christ.

Paul recalls the dedicated manner in which these women worked with him in the Gospel. He calls them, literally fellow-*athletes*, implying agonizing struggles midst perilous times, not only with Paul but with each other.

Then Paul thinks of other members of the team. Clement and those whose names he does not need to mention for they are described in the Book of Life. What happy memories flood Paul's mind. He would like the team intact again. He is saying, "Get those two ladies back on the team!"

These worthy women should not be allowed to perpetuate their misbegotten misery. Paul wishes them reconciled so that they will be remembered for their devoted, meritòrious service. It seems likely that the beloved apostle's plea was not in vain.

An unknown poet expresses what we hope occurred in their case:

> They walked with God in peace and love,
> But failed with one another;
> While sternly for the Faith they strove,
> Sister fell out with sister;
> But He in whom they put their trust,
> Who knew their frames that they were dust,
> Pitied and healed their weaknesses.
>
> He found them in His house of prayer,
> With one accord assembled;
> And so revealed His presence there,
> They wept with joy and trembled;
> One cup they drank, one bread they brake,
> One baptism shared, one language spake,
> Forgiving and forgiven.

Then forth they went with tongues of flame
In one blest theme uniting;
The love of Jesus and His Name,
God's children all uniting;
That love our theme and watchword still,
The law of love may we fulfill,
And love as we are love.

11
Curing the Boss-Complex

Sons of Bosses is an organization of young men who have taken over control of family businesses or are in line for the top job because of heredity. Such men seem to have special problems: often their fathers are intensely competitive, viewing successor sons as threats or embarrassments, not welcome associates. Some fathers want to keep running the show when their sons have become better qualified. Yet some sons want supreme authority before they are capable of exercising it. The truth is, human nature—whether paternal or filial—relishes control over people.

This spirit does not avoid the church. First-century Diotrephes was such a man. The Apostle John wrote a congregation these words about this officious character in their midst:

"I wrote unto the church, but Diotrephes, who loveth to have the preeminence among them, receiveth us not. Wherefore, if I come, I will remember his deeds which he doeth, prating against us with malicious words; and not content therewith, neither doth he himself receive the brethren, and forbiddeth them that would, and casteth them out of the church" (3 John 9-10).

Leader Versus Boss

Management experts describe the various styles of leadership as bureaucratic—operating by rules and regulations; laissez faire—permissive; participative—others sharing in decisions; and dictatorial—one-man rule. No question about Diotrephes' mode—he was an iron-fisted autocrat.

We must distinguish between bossism and leadership. Every church needs leaders with the gift of government who have vision, set goals, implement these objectives, and see them through to completion—perhaps stirring up a few waves in the process. But this isn't bossism. Leaders who share authority may be outvoted, but a boss demands his way regardless of opposition. Diotrephes not only told everyone else what to do, he opposed the very teaching of Christ. The Apostle John indicates drastic action is necessary.

A letter John had written this church about some itinerant preachers had fallen into the hands of Diotrephes, likely because he was an officer. Magnifying his authority, he haughtily refused to receive these travelers, an insult to the apostle whom they represented. John then wrote the well-loved Gaius, whose godly walk and generous hospitality were well known, to ask him to welcome these visitors.

John accuses Diotrephes of "prating," a word that occurs only here in the New Testament. It carries the idea of boiling up hollow bubbles. A related adjective is translated "tattlers." His pretentious words characterized him as a wicked windbag. Somehow succeeding in getting the majority under his thumb, Diotrephes excommunicated those who opposed him.

How often in history the man with top authority has resented the presence of even a loyal second-in-command. Richard Wolff in *Man At The Top* asks, "Is this what happened to the French Premier Pompidou in May 1968? Was he fired by General DeGaulle because the Premier had become too popular? Pompidou kept the government running during the May riots in 1968. Pompidou masterminded the campaign which brought DeGaulle back into power. His reward was to be dismissed. His success became a threat to DeGaulle. Willful and arbitrary, DeGaulle acted in true autocratic fashion, retaining a firm grip on the levers of power" (pp. 108-109).

Church officers have sometimes thwarted attempts to place on a board or committee a person whose achievements and talents might endanger that officer's supremacy. Even pastors have arranged for the departure of assistants whose ability and popularity became a threat to their own eminence. The love of power is not far behind love for money in subverting character.

Diotrephes is described as one "who loveth to have the preeminence." In the original language, *preeminence* is a compound word meaning "to love to be first." This compound is found only here in the New Testament. The second word of the compound, *to be first*, is used in Colossians 1:18, referring to Christ: "that in all things He might have the preeminence." Diotrephes was guilty of dangerous presumption.

Diotrephes is the archetype of vain, self-seeking, self-elected overseers who are obsessed with lording it over their brethren and browbeating all who get in their way. He was the forerunner of the "church boss," a type known wherever the Church has gone. Every church seems to have one.

Greek language scholar A. T. Robertson once wrote an article on Diotrephes for a church magazine, portraying him as one who wants to control a church according to his own whims. Subsequently 20 deacons from various parts of the country wrote the editor to cancel their subscriptions because of this "personal attack" made on them!

How should a church boss be handled? The directions in chapter 9 dealing with brothers-at-odds should be followed. A person offended by the overbearing bossism of a church leader should schedule a private appointment to face the dominating personality with evidence of his oppressive conduct. If the attempt makes no dent on the self-styled boss, the person offended must seek additional witnesses who agree on a need for change in behavior. If a second confrontation produces no remorse, the matter should be taken to the congregation. At that point the church will have to choose the kind of leadership it wants.

That Boss Within

Though a Diotrephes should be dealt with swiftly and firmly, a more pertinent problem in most churches is how to overcome the spirit of bossism in our own lives. We need to counteract the chief syndrome that dissipates our energy in recognition-seeking rather than in getting God's work done.

One firm has made headlines out of deflating a person's ego. It signed contracts to provide a pie and have it thrown by one of its employees into the face of a pompous victim or thick-skinned friend. In its first few months over 60 hits were made on disbelieving victims at a minimum of $35 per splash. Imagine the surprise of a dignified executive waiting for an elevator when a stranger whips a pie out of a cardboard box and mashes it into his astonished face, giving the pie a professional twist at impact, sending the goo meandering down face and droppng off the chin onto immaculate shirt and tie! A member of the company said, "A pie in the face brings a man's dignity down to where it should be, and puts the big guys on the same level with everyone else." But a more likely result is a raging court suit or repayment in kind!

The New Testament suggests several helps for overcoming Diotrephes-like self-centeredness—and with God all things are possible!

Consider others as worthy of greater honor. Delicate situations arise in churches when we feel we aren't getting our rightful position, privilege, or prestige. Some less-deserving person is given a prominent seat on the platform; someone is not asked to do a job for which he thinks he has the ability; another is asked to serve on a choice committee; or our service is not noticed and commended. The New Testament reply is, "in honor preferring one another'' (Rom. 12:10). And, ''In lowliness of mind let each esteem other better than themselves'' (Phil. 2:3).

Jesus counseled His followers not to claim honor by choosing their own place at a dinner. He seems to teach that we should not deliberately seek the top spot, large ministry, or bright limelight. Building bigger ecclesiastical empires or accepting an important position because it is strategic and influential may cultivate a Diotrephes mentality. Theologian Francis Schaeffer has said we should consciously take the lowest place unless the Lord Himself forces us into a more responsible one. Otherwise we may find ourselves ''over our depth'' with ensuing difficulties that cause unrest of soul and decrease of spiritual power.

Schaeffer also points out in *No Little People* that there are no ''big people'' and no ''little people'' in God's sight, just dedicated and undedicated people. The seemingly little is big if that is where God wants us. Two little girls built a shack for a clubhouse in their backyard, then scribbled on the wall these perceptive rules: (1) Nobody act big. (2) Nobody act small. (3) Everybody act medium.

German author Goethe and composer Beethoven were out walking. Wherever they went people pointed them out, and Goethe exclaimed, ''Isn't it maddening? I simply cannot escape this homage!'' Beethoven replied, ''Don't be too much distressed by it; it is just possible that some of it may be for me.''

How different from the attitude of Principal Cairns, headmaster of an English school. As a member of a group assigned to sit at the front of a great gathering, he walked onto the platform in a line with the other dignitaries. His appearance was met by a burst of applause, and Cairns stepped back to let the man behind pass him, then began to applaud his colleague. In his modesty he assumed the applause was for another. He may have a prominent place at Jesus' table.

Submit one to another. This is one manifestation of being filled with the Holy Spirit (Eph. 5:18-21). Under the wrong kind of spirits men become self-assertive; under the Holy Spirit's influence become humble.

John Owen, one-time Chancellor of Oxford University, used to go to hear the unschooled John Bunyan preach when the tinker came to London. King Charles II expressed surprise that so learned a person would listen to so uneducated a man as Bunyan. Owen replied, "Had I the tinker's abilities, please your Majesty, I should gladly relinquish my learning."

Submission is voluntary accommodation to another, displaying modesty, humility, unwillingness to unnecessarily dispute, gentleness, forbearance, contentment. Such an attitude reduces the friction of human interaction and contributes greatly to a church's peace and unity. No one, including pastors, should be exempt from accountability to some other person, board, or committee. Each committee member should submit his ideas to the judgment of the rest of his committee members. Where there is submission on both sides of an issue, there is not debasement, but union. In an era of independent action, how needed is a reminder of the importance of mutual subordination to fellow believers.

A newspaper item captioned "The Principle of the Thing" told how stubbornness had caused a split in Japan's Stubbornness Club, formed a year earlier by 20 people who considered themselves obstinate but who wanted to be constructive members of society. Their monthly meetings became so clamorous that the vice-president resigned to form a more discreet Society for the Preservation of Stubbornness.

Too often church splits are caused by stubborn Christians who hold tenaciously to their own opinions in secondary matters. Though claiming to hold to "the principles" of the matter, they are more likely defending their own prestige and personal views, unwilling to submit to one another lovingly.

Serve one another. At the annual homecomings of William and Mary College in Virginia, a number of prominent people, including a college president, a famous governor, and well-known business and professional leaders are seen wearing white jackets. The jackets signify that these men earned all or much of their way through college by waiting on tables. The New Testament asks all believers to join the "Christian order of the white jackets" when it urges: "By love serve one another" (Gal. 5:13).

Jesus' disciples displayed the Diotrephes syndrome on at least three occasions by arguing about which of them would have top spot in His coming kingdom. The first time Jesus' response was to place a child before them and exhort the disciples to childlike humility (Mark 9:33-37).

On the second occasion, Jesus pointed out that secular leaders sought the number one position in order to wield power, but in Christ's circle the leader needs the opposite motive. "Whosoever will be great among you, shall be your minister; and whosoever of you will be the chiefest, shall be servant of all." Then to contrast the selfish aspirations of His disciples, Jesus gave the example of His own service. "For even the Son of man came not to be ministered unto, but to minister, and to give His life a ransom for many" (Mark 10:43-45).

The third instance occurred in the Upper Room with the Saviour's death less than 24 hours away. The disciples were debating who should rank the highest in the coming kingdom when they should have been competing to extend the courtesy of footwashing. Though basin and towel had been provided, no aspiring leader would abdicate his throne of hoped-for preeminence to kneel before his subjects. As they looked away from towel and basin with studied indifference, the amazing happened. Jesus rose to give a graphic demonstration that should have forever dulled their lust for leadership. The Lord of Glory, at whose beck legions of angels would immediately respond, chose the servant's place and took the soiled feet of the disciples in His own hands. "If I then, your Lord and Master, have washed your feet; ye also ought to wash one another's feet" (John 13:14). His action told

His followers to seek service, not sovereignty. He made forever noble the order of the white jackets.

Surprisingly, all three recorded disputes among the disciples as to who should be greatest, occurred right after Jesus had spoken of His coming death and future kingdom glory. Somehow their thoughts slid past the Cross to dwell on the kingdom splendor, making them ask for positions of honor in that glorious realm.

But even for us, who have a nineteen-century vantage point, how quickly after private devotions or communion service do our minds divert from the supreme sacrifice of Christ to our own importance, our rights, our dignity, our position, our authority! When tempted to thoughts of preeminence, to having our own way in the church, we need to turn to Calvary to behold the Servant of servants whose whole life was one continuous ministry, not bossing, but giving His very lifeblood in one final and supreme gift to others. Earnest meditation on the cross of Jesus should quell our desire for domination.

When I survey the wondrous cross
On which the Prince of Glory died,
My richest gain I count but loss,
And pour contempt on all my pride.
—Isaac Watts

12
More Than Conquerors

Mark Twain once wrote, tongue-in-cheek, about two cages. In the first was placed a cat, to which were added some doves, then a dog, then a rabbit, a fox, a goose, a squirrel, and finally a monkey. In the other cage was placed an Irish Catholic from Tipperary, a Scots Presbyterian from Aberdeen, a Turk, a Greek Christian, an Armenian, a Methodist, a Buddhist, a Brahman, and then a Salvation Army colonel. Two days later the animals were living in peace—but the second cage was a "chaos of gory odds and ends of turbans and fezzes and plaids and bones and flesh—not a specimen alive."

According to Mark Twain, the animals with higher reasoning had fought over a theological detail, then "carried the matter to a higher court." The famous humorist thus gained another of his laughs at the expense of religion.

Though believers are to contend for the faith, they are not to be contentious. Too often fighting and feuding lead to mutual destruction. The church at Galatia, volatile by nature, must have been in danger of ecclesiastical cannibalism, for Paul warned them: "But if ye bite and devour one another, take heed that ye be not consumed one of another" (Gal. 5:15).

We pointed out earlier that church controversies fall into two categories: substantive (over ideas) and interpersonal (because of personality clashes). This chapter will deal with the latter type, especially its root causes.

Much church conflict arises when believers become petty, personal, and pugnacious with other believers. Instead of attacking the issue, they assault each other with their tongues. A study of causes of pastoral drop-out reveals that a high percentage of preachers who leave the ministry within five years of ordination do so because their idealism has been worn thin by frustrating encounters with church members who are stubborn, selfish, and immature. Parishioners, instead of dealing with the problem, dissect the people with whom they disagree!

The source of interpersonal strife is usually our sinful desires. James asks, "What is the source of quarrels and conflict among you?" A rather shocking question to members of the body of Christ, addressed in the salutation as "my brethren" (4:1; 1:2, NASB). James immediately answers his question by identifying the cause as "your pleasures that wage war in your members" (NASB). Some of these combative desires are expressed in disparagement, envy, and denunciation.

Disparagement

Someone suggested that Adam and Eve must have had a hard time making conversation when they had no one to talk about. Someone has said that the quality of conversation, in descending rank, is about *ideas*, then *things*, then *people*.

James says it simply "Speak not evil of one another, brethren" (4:11). It's a matter of harshly judging even when not knowing the significant facts.

Judging takes many forms: knocking, mudslinging, gossip, jumping at conclusions, backbiting, slandering, caustically criticizing. By judging, we not only usurp the prerogative of God who alone knows all the facts, but we may do irreparable harm to fellow believer. A teenager who accepted Christ at a meeting talked with a Christian youth on his way home who voiced an ugly criticism of the preacher. The new convert showed no subsequent interest in the church.

Roast beef makes a good Sunday dinner, but not roast preacher. Many children, hearing their parents rend the pastor at Sunday meals, have later refused to listen to him either in public preaching or private counsel. Neither should we serve roast Sunday School teacher, roast organist, or roast soloist. We cannot build up the Lord's work while tearing down His workers.

How easy to misjudge. A pastor tells how he noticed one of his Sunday School teachers absent from most of the church services, though always present to teach his class. The pastor made a critical remark to the superintendent who answered, "Pastor, you're fairly new here. You probably haven't been able to visit his house. Make a visit, then let me know what you think." When the pastor made the visit, his heart was deeply moved. That teacher had an invalid child at home, so pitiful it would melt the heart. Comments the pastor, "Now instead of criticizing him, I admire him as one of the finest Christians I know."

Though a little thing, the untamed tongue has crushed hearts, divided families, and split churches. John Wesley, father of Methodism, drew up the following proposition for his followers:

—they were not to listen to, or willingly inquire after, any ill concerning each other;

—if they heard any ill of each other, they were not to be eager to believe it;

—as soon as possible they were to contact the person concerned, by speaking or writing;

—till this was done, they were not to write or speak a syllable of it to any other person, not to mention it thereafter, unless conscience obliged otherwise.

Because criticism begets criticism, quarrels can easily escalate nto feuds. That's why we have to be very careful when we see ›omething in church we don't like. We should ask the Lord,

"Should I make mention of this? Should I put a note on the registration card or in the suggestion box?" Says the writer of Proverbs, "It is hard to stop a quarrel once it starts, so don't let it begin" (17:14, LB).

When a gossip approached a wise old deacon with, "What's going on ?" he replied, "I am."

Envy

A cardinal vice that plays havoc with interpersonal relationships is envy. Paul said, "Let us not be desirous of vain glory . . .envying one another" (Gal. 5:26).

Though pride was later positioned first on the list of "seven deadly sins," envy had this dubious distinction in the evaluation of the early church fathers.

Envy has been defined as ill-will toward a person because of his superiority. Because malice (ill-will) is part of its essence, envy may have destructive influence on our fellow believers. Envy is pain, grief, annoyance, or displeasure toward a person whom we deem superior to us in position, power, proficiency, possessions, or popularity, thus involving a certain degree of malignity. This malice may be expressed in our thoughts: "I wish he'd fall flat on his face." While sympathy makes us "rejoice with them that do rejoice, and weep with them that weep" (Rom. 12:15), envy causes us to rejoice when others weep and weep when others rejoice. Envy is that nasty gratification when you learn that your fellow believer's new car has a dented fender (and you wish it were both fenders), or that his business isn't doing well, or that his brilliant child failed to win a scholarship.

Envy may express itself not only in our thinking but in our speaking, prompting name-calling, sinister insinuations, or devilish detractions. Many idle words spring from envy. When someone makes a substantial gift to the church, the envious speculates: "He's trying to escape the income tax." After a lovely soprano solo a jealous choir member reflects, "Oh-oh, she's not hitting those high notes so well."

A Christian couple buys a new car and new furniture, and a fellow church member comments, "I don't know how they do it. Probably they don't tithe. We'd have a lot more money to spend if we didn't tithe."

Someone wrote this doggerel:

I hate the guys
Who minimize and criticize
The other guys
Whose enterprise
Has made them rise
Above the guys who criticize.

Poisonous ponderings may lead not only to venomous villification but also wicked works. When Isaac's possessions increased, envious Philistines filled his wells with dirt. Envy made Joseph's brothers sell him into slavery. King Saul's insane jealousy harassed David into a seven-year exile. Because of a plot by envious governors, Daniel was thrown into the lion's den. Most heinous of all, envy put Christ on the cross, for "Pilate knew that for envy they had delivered him" (Matt. 27:18).

Not only should we not envy, but neither should we provoke another to envy. Mother Rebekah's favoritism of son Jacob, and Isaac's for Esau, caused a family fight. Perhaps Jacob erred seriously by making Joseph a coat of many colors and placing him in a supervisory capacity. No wonder "when his brethren saw that their father loved him more than all his brethren, they hated him, and could not speak peaceably unto him" (Gen. 37:4), and later stripped him of his many-colored coat.

Often Christians unconsciously stir up envy by flaunting possessions or achievements. One Christian spoke often of the accomplishments of his son, his degrees and honors, which galled some listening parents into jealousy. One woman frequently mentioned in the women's fellowship her summer home, furs, expensive jewelry, and round-the-world trip to the mission fields, arousing envy. Those who refer repeatedly to their fortunes, feats, fame, family, and fun may irk hearers into wishing to see them lowered a few pegs. This subconscious animosity sets the stage for interpersonal conflicts in the church.

Don't flash your advantages, real or imaginary, before others. Such vaunting may challenge to envious combat. Paul cautions us not to be "provoking one another" (Gal. 5:26). Rather, if we are going to agitate folks, we should provoke them upward to edification. Much more noble is it to inspire people to emulate graces of Christian character.

Denunciation

A man bitten by a dog became violently ill, goes a story. The doctor explained, "You've been bitten by a rabid dog and you are dying of hydrophobia. There's nothing I can do for you." The stricken man asked for a pencil and paper, then spent several hours thinking and writing. On a return visit the doctor remarked, "You certainly are making a lengthy will." Retorted the patient, "I'm not making my will; I'm making a list of people I'm going to bite."

Paul warns believers against "biting" one another. Great and godly as were the church reformers of the 16th century, they were guilty of heaping invective on opponents among fellow believers. Philip Schaff, a careful historian, described Martin Luther's debating disposition thus. His "writings smell of powder; his words are battles; he overwhelms his opponents with a roaring cannonade of argument, eloquence, passion, and abuse."

Luther insulted Zwingli by deliberately and repeatedly misspelling his name. He piled such vulgarity on him that Schaff said he could not translate its meaning into decent English. That such verbal abuse was commonplace in his day did not make it innocent and harmless.

In an old monastery in Germany may be seen two pairs of

antlers interlocked, said to be found in that position many years ago. The deer had been fighting when their antlers got jammed together and could not be separated. They died with locked horns. Said one historian, "I would like to take those horns into every house and school in the country." And we would add, "And into every church."

How tragic that members of the same body could be linked for mutual destruction. Does any part of the human body fight against any other member? Does hand pluck out eye, or leg kick ankle? When General Stonewall Jackson heard his men cutting each other down over what strategy to use in the conflict, he interjected: "Remember, gentlemen, the enemy is over there," pointing in the direction of the battle that was then raging.

Fighting among believers carries a high price tag. Just as in war both victor and vanquished pay a tremendous price, so battle among brethren scatters spiritual casualties indiscriminately. Offensive language, envy, and unkind behavior destroy friendships, tear down reputations, and decimate the church. It seems incredible to us today that the Reformers actually drowned Anabaptists because the latter insisted so strongly that baptism was only for believers!

Two little sisters had a nasty spat, and their mother told them this story. Once upon a time were two cats: one black with a white tip on his black tail and the other white with the tip of his tail black. Said the mother, "These cats were always fighting. When the white cat lay sleeping cozily before the fire, and the black cat entered the room, up would leap the white cat with back arched and tail fluffed out, hissing and spitting and calling the black cat all kinds of names. He acted exactly like two little girls I know."

Joyce and Jean looked at each other, but mother went on as if she hadn't noticed. "One day some of the boys saw the cats fighting in the backyard. They tied the two cats together by the ends of their tails, hung them over the clothesline, and left them.

By morning they'll have their fill of fighting, thought the boys. But when the boys came back in the morning, there was nothing left but the tips of two tails, one black and the other white. They had eaten each other up!"

"O mother," giggled Joyce. "They couldn't have done that! How could they keep eating without any mouths?"

"No," agreed mother, "they couldn't, of course. That's just a story. But little girls sometimes say biting things to each other, until they've left nothing good of each other at all. For instance, each of you has said tonight that the other was selfish; and worse than that, that the other was lying. So you've 'eaten up' each other's unselfishness and truthfulness. This afternoon I heard you say, 'You mean thing!' So your kindness is eaten up, too. I'm afraid that some day I'll find no goodness left in my girls. It will all be eaten up—just badness left."

Vindictiveness does tend toward extinction for all participants. Strife shakes the sanctuary. Chris Lyons, pastor of the Wheaton (Ill.) Bible Church said in a sermon on James 4, "I know of churches which had a great testimony and where many were saved, but conflict came in. The church split. And never again through the years has that been a great church nor had many people saved. These churches go on for a generation with all the scars and hurts; they seem never to get over it."

God never promised to bless a church divided through interpersonal strife. This is why believers must strive to keep the unity of the Spirit. When someone steps on our toes, intrudes into an area not his business, or something happens over which we could easily blow our top or quit the church, we have to exercise great self-control to keep peace.

All-Conquering Love

In the verse before the warning against consuming one another, Paul reminds, "You shall love your neighbor as yourself" (Gal. 5:14). Malice consumes, but love conserves, turning incipient friction into cementing fellowship. And, when the outside world sees compassion among Christians, they become convinced of the genuineness of Christianity. As Jesus said, "By this shall all men know that ye are My disciples" (John 13:35). Fortunately, some churches have proved the truth and power of this reality.

Early one Monday morning some years ago Pastor Virgil Savage of the First Baptist Church of Redmond, Oregon, sensed trouble when he answered his phone. His Sunday School superintendent, voice irritated and insistent, said, "There's something I want to talk to you about in your study this morning."

When his 6′3″, 200-pound superintendent showed up a few minutes later, the pastor could tell all was not well. The superintendent had some personal matters between them that needed airing. Settling their differences in a Christian manner, they had prayer together. Then Pastor Savage suggested they meet for prayer the next morning.

They began to meet regularly. Other men asked to join. Thus began a daily men's 6:30 A.M. prayer meeting which was to result in the winning of many men to Christ. One convert was the town butcher, Dan Lawler, a cigar-chewing, whiskey-drinking merchant who was proud of his combination meat market and cold-storage locker business. Soon cigar and whiskey disappeared from Lawler's life, while a growing interest in the Bible led him to sell his flourishing business and move to Portland to attend Bible institute and seminary.

A burden for starting a new church in an unchurched area led him to found the Gateway Baptist Church. Then he felt the burden for starting another church. Through his leadership during the next several years 17 building projects were completed with the aid of involved laymen. Lawler's talents were invested statewide as he served for years as director of church extension for the Conservative Baptist Association of Oregon. The urge to plant another new church led him back to pioneer what has become another fast-growing church.

Interestingly, the man who took over the first church he started, Gateway Baptist, was none other than the Sunday School superintendent, one of the original pair who started the prayer meeting.

It all came about as a result of two men meeting to solve their differences, and then joining in fellowship and prayer.

The psalmist said, "Behold, how good and how pleasant it is for brethren to dwell together in unity!" (Ps. 133:1)

The way to win those inevitable church fights is to *give in—to the Holy Spirit*, and watch Him restore unity and power to the Church.